YES YOU!
YES NOW!
LEADERSHIP

"Within the complex and dynamic environment of flying, safety depends upon teamwork from a fluid, but defined command structure. Dr. Tarr's examination of leadership is an insightful perspective on what makes my cockpit work; as well as what makes an individual and a culture successful. He gives an entertaining and enlightening picture of the symbiotic relationship of leading and following. Everybody will enjoy and take something away from this book, from the quote in every chapter to the story that makes it come alive."

— *Steve Speight, commercial jet pilot and former Navy flier*

"My years as a student, teacher, player, and coach have taught me the value of leadership and the often overlooked value of followership. I've been in both roles, constructively supporting and questioning my superiors while expecting my team to do the same for me. Through thought-provoking quotes and engaging stories, Dr. Tarr has shown what anyone can do to achieve greater success by being a yes-you yes-now leader."

— Pat Bangasser, high school teacher and coach

Yes You! Yes Now! Leadership

ॐॐ

The No Excuses Path to Success
By
Leading Yourself
Leading Your Team
Leading Your Leader

Dr. Steven C. Tarr

Columbia-Capstone

Yes You! Yes Now! Leadership, with or without punctuation, is a trademark of
Columbia-Capstone

Published by Columbia-Capstone, Redmond, Washington
www.columbia-capstone.com

Pyramid of Success is used with permission from John Wooden and can be
seen in its entirety in his books and at www.CoachJohnWooden.com

Cover design by Brion Sausser, www.bookcreatives.com

ISBN-13: 978-0-9821148-0-3
ISBN-10: 0-9821148-0-X

Library of Congress Control Number: 2008909544
Library of Congress subject headings
    Leadership.
    Followership.
    Teams in the workplace -- Management.
    Emotional intelligence.
    Work and family.

To my wonderful children, Emily and David.
They are incredibly intelligent, compassionate people who have taught
me so much as their lives have unfolded.

And to Coach John Wooden for his willingness to share his wisdom
about doing the right things for the right reasons.

Contents

Leading Your Team

Leading Your Leader

Conclusion

Foreword

Many people like to see themselves as the leader but as Dr. Tarr points out, the reality is that we spend most of our time following, though often ineffectively. Even the most forthright leader is true to his or her own beliefs and goals, with the same diligence and dedication that he or she expects others to have. Dr. Tarr's book is an enlightened view of the much neglected subject of effective following, by making the choice that you can lead right now, with no excuses. This simple but powerful concept touches the lives of everyone involved in any organization, work, family, or team. If you are in a position of leadership you will learn to recognize the qualities needed in your team to make your leadership effective.

If you aspire to lead you will learn how to improve your chances through the effective support of your current leaders. If you wish to solidify your position in your organization you will learn how to maximize your contribution through high impact and effective following. If all three are applicable, and for many they are, then this book is thrice the insightful read.

James Dixon
Chief Executive Officer
Greythorn North America

Preface

You can make things better now! A formal leader sets direction and rallies people to the cause but doesn't and can't do everything. They depend on other people to do the bulk of the work, people who enable themselves by thinking, "I can take action and I can take it immediately." These people remove excuses and make things happen by practicing yes-you yes-now leadership.

When your team, family, or work group are trying to achieve something, only one person has formal leadership at any given moment. Everyone else follows. The effective followers understand their roles and use them with a sense of immediacy to help their team reach their goals.

In fact, most of us don't have formal leadership titles most of the time. As you'll find throughout the chapters of this book, we may flash into a leadership role and then resume our follower role. You'll see this as you watch a group in action. The coach or boss may say something, then another team member will lead the next step. The dynamics are never-ending and the power is immense through yes-you yes-now leadership, no matter what formal role you hold.

When I first thought about this I wondered why some people were good followers and some were not. I searched for books or seminars on the topic of following and found very little. Most of the references were about leadership, what a leader should do to lead followers. What I wanted was some information on how a follower can help his or her leader and teammates make progress towards their goals. There really wasn't much.

I began researching the topic of followers and found a lot on religious and cult followers, a smattering on political followers, and a little bit on formal follower roles. I wanted something readable, accessible, and positive. I started keeping track of behaviors I had observed or read about which either helped or hindered a team's progress. These turned into the points made at the beginning of each chapter, which are illustrated by colorful historical events as well as stories from everyday life.

Formal leaders get all the attention. Turning yourself into one is overly emphasized by authors, the media, and the public. But followers are the ones who really make the world go round by practicing yes-you yes-now leadership.

Just as there are bad leaders and good leaders, there are bad followers and good followers. Bad leaders and bad followers are often focused on themselves. In their quest for power, they have more tactics than the rest of us have. Why? Because they use tactics most people reject, such as lying and cheating.

Yes-you yes-now leadership helps anyone wanting to effectively reach team goals – including good leaders and good followers. These people have the skills to achieve those goals by working with honesty, integrity, and decency. With many of us in a follower role much of the time, learning to use yes-you yes-now leadership is critical to making your team succeed and to attaining that success for everyone. The stories that follow will help teach these skills.

⤙⤚

No work such as this can be completed by only one person and there are many people who contributed to this book. Some of them exhibited the prime characteristics of a yes-you yes-now leader and their stories are told on the pages that follow. Some of them know who they are. Some names are real and some have been changed to ensure their privacy. In all cases, thank you to these special people.

I would also like to acknowledge my editor, Carolyn Schott, for her dedication to the spirit of the book. Her comments were almost always causing me to think, "Why didn't I see that?" Of course that's what great editors do by helping writers when we can no longer see straight. Thank you, Carolyn, for your help bringing this book to life.

And lastly, thank you to Cyndie Fox whose attention to detail greatly improved the final quality. Her desire to see this book in print, so other people can empower themselves with its principles, helped push me forward.

I appreciate all the help I have received from so many people.

Steve Tarr
Redmond, Washington
January, 2009

YES YOU!
YES NOW!
LEADERSHIP

The Basics

The Yes-You Yes-Now Leader

"Leadership flows from the minds of followers more than from the titles of leaders, more from the perception of willing followers than from anointment."[1]

—*Lance Secretan, master teacher and former ambassador to the United Nations Environment Program*

Most simply, a yes-you yes-now leader is a person who wants success and shares in the goals of others. This person may be just like you: not the formal leader but smart, full of good ideas, and often in a follower role. Being a follower does not imply any sort of power hierarchy, though neither does it exclude it. This can be a boss/worker or coach/player relationship, but is often a more subtle relationship among a group of equals. In each of these cases, the success of the group comes first and foremost and is used to guide every decision for the individuals and the group.

അഃ⊷

The Chicago Bulls of the National Basketball Association (NBA) dominated professional basketball in the 1990s. During that incredible run, they were playing a critical game and the score was very close. As time on the clock ran down, Coach Phil Jackson called a time-out to set up a play. One of the players for the Bulls at the time was Scotty Pippen, a key ingredient in the teams that had won six NBA titles in eight years. The play Coach

Jackson drew up did not call for Pippen to take the shot because their opponents expected Pippen to take it. Instead, a teammate, Tony Kukoc, was to shoot, with Pippen acting as a decoy. In disgust, Pippen refused to return to the court at the end of the timeout despite the packed house and a national television audience. Widespread media reports said he wanted and deserved the last shot. He wanted to be the hero. But it was Kukoc who did what his coach and team needed – while Pippen sat on the bench.

Were Pippen's actions supporting the success of the team? He was certainly capable of hitting a last-minute shot but it is very clear that his dissent was a distraction at that point in the game. To refuse to re-enter the game was essentially an act of quitting on the team.

A person practicing yes-you yes-now leadership speaks and acts for the good of the team in pursuit of team goals, regardless of their own personal goals. There is much more to celebrate in the team winning the game than in any one person demanding to take the shot. And yes, Kukoc made the shot and the Bulls won the game. He wasn't the head coach but at that moment he was the team leader on the court. He was a shining example of yes-you yes-now leadership.

Ask Questions, Seek Understanding

"Some people will never learn anything, because they understand everything too soon."[2]

—*Alexander Pope, English poet*

Early in my career I made a point to separate teamwork and friendship because I felt that the demands of making good team decisions would be compromised by the strong desire of wanting to help out a work-friend for non-work reasons, thus undermining the team.

By keeping these separate, I developed a strong ability to focus on the team for the good of the whole. I still cared very much for the individual, but I would not let that color my judgment. People used to tell me that they could not imagine how I could coach my own children in basketball and treat them like any other team member. But I believed my role was to help each player the best way I could. So why would I favor my children or any other children? My role was to understand the player's situation and develop their ability to perform on their own merits. Empathy is very important for a yes-you yes-now leader, so I had to understand what they were experiencing in order to give them, and all players, the proper guidance.

It's not always easy to understand what people need, so I have lived by and coached others to live by a simple saying: "Ask questions, seek understanding." Its corollary is, of course, "Provide answers, share information."

⌇⌇⌇

There are many examples in our own lives to show how understanding, or lack of it, affects our beliefs and our actions. Why did that driver just zip in front of you in traffic? What a jerk! Or maybe they are late for an appointment or don't know the road. We can't know, so we need to resist the temptation to assume the worst. Ask questions, seek understanding, even of yourself.

When Julio Feliciano started missing school at Mount Tahoma High School in Tacoma, Washington, the school administrators figured he was just skipping out like so many other high-schoolers do. He fit the stereotype they'd seen so many times before. When he was absent they figured he was probably hanging out somewhere, maybe causing trouble for someone.

But not only was he staying out of trouble, he was doing some good – for his sick mother who was home ill with AIDS. There were days when she was too weak to feed herself and needed help eating.

When Julio's school counselor, Dave Osterhaus, discovered Julio's real story, his perspective immediately changed from one of suspicion to one of compassion. And his approach to helping Julio changed with it. Osterhaus adjusted Julio's academic schedule to be more flexible so he could keep up with school and help his mother. As word spread throughout the school, Julio was no longer treated with suspicion, but with sympathy and concern.

About a year later, Julio's mother passed away. Amid the sadness of that event, the more suitable academic schedule enabled Julio to keep his grades up and to earn a Gates Achievement Scholarship to attend college. Osterhaus' new-found understanding had helped him be a positive force in Julio's life and had helped Julio make it to college.

Such understanding helps even the accomplished and famous. Professional golfer Tom Watson won one U.S. Open, two Masters titles, and five British Opens. For most of his thirty-some years on the pro tour, he showed few feelings and shared little information with others. He was also considered to be a hidden man, lacking in emotions and a human face to go along with his golfing ability. He never appeared to want to understand what was happening in his friends' lives, his caddie's life, nor his children's lives.

He had been married for over 25 years, but that fell apart. He was so consumed with golf and hunting that he had barely been a force in raising his now adult children. His caddie, Bruce Edwards, who had stuck with him for almost his entire pro career, worked to smooth out some of the wrinkles by helping Watson whenever he could.

Then one day the tables turned. Edwards was diagnosed with ALS, also known as Lou Gehrig's disease. The man who had always understood what made Tom Watson tick was now in need of help and understanding himself. He called Watson and shared the news. Edwards didn't ask for it, but Watson immediately offered help, saying they would beat the disease even though no one ever had.

Suddenly Watson understood what someone else needed. Since that time, he has used his famous name to promote research on ALS and call on doctors world-wide to get information for Edwards. In one year alone, his fundraisers took in $3 million for ALS research and he donated one million dollars of his own.[3]

His awareness of what Edwards needed helped him become aware of what others in his life needed. He stopped drinking, cold turkey. He made repeated sincere efforts to mend the relationships with his children, despite a less-than-friendly divorce from their mother. He finally realized that so many years had passed by, wondering where the time had gone, and most importantly, how much time was left for his friend.

Looking back over their long friendship, Edwards said the best times were in the early 1980s when Watson was winning and it seemed like they would win together forever. But Watson said the best times were helping Edwards. "Back then it was always about me. Winning for yourself and winning for somebody else, you can't compare the two."

Watson had been the golfing team leader for so many years, but with Edwards's illness, he rose up to become a yes-you yes-now leader. He learned to ask questions. And he learned how to understand what his teammate needed. Just as the teacher, Dave Osterhaus, began to understand and help Julio Feliciano.

Ask questions, seek understanding.

A Beacon to Guide You

"Something magical happens when you bring together a group of people from different disciplines with a common purpose."[4]

—Mark Stefik, author and scientist

It's hard to be a yes-you yes-now leader without knowing the beacon you're using for navigation. Throughout thick and thin, what keeps a person on course? It is often said and it is often true, that people are loyal to a leader. This is a fatal mistake that begs the question, to what is the leader loyal? What is the leader's lighthouse? It is often a cause and seldom a person or a group of people. Without reciprocal personal loyalty, the relationships are bound to disintegrate.

More enduring guidance is best found in the purpose itself. All members of the team are thus focused on the pursuit and attainment of the goal, providing a solid basis for success and the deep interdependent relationships that come with it. This is a tricky concept because it can be difficult to separate the purpose from a person whose very essence embodies that purpose.

This is most apparent when the leader leaves the team.

❧

Bobby Knight became famous in his Indiana red sweaters. His passion for basketball was as vivid as the sweaters. But his passionate and infamous temper tantrums overshadowed his considerable coaching talent. When Indiana University President Myles Brand saw the established zero-tolerance limit for unruly behavior exceeded, he fired Knight.

A number of players threatened to quit the team. Knight's assistant, Mike Davis, was the heir apparent as head coach, but was directly lobbied by Knight to pass up the job. Knight wanted to inflict further damage after, in his opinion, being unfairly dumped. Knight's loyalty was to himself and he wished for Davis also to be loyal to him.

But Davis accepted when he was offered the job of interim head coach at Indiana. As much as Knight had taught him, as much as he respected Knight as a coach and mentor, his loyalty was to Indiana University with the purpose of rebuilding the program to a high level of competitiveness.

The more powerful and enduring loyalty to a purpose superseded his personal loyalty to Knight. He could not turn the job down. Even though Coach Knight was the leader and catalyst of the Indiana basketball program, Indiana basketball itself was a larger purpose.

The story had not one, but two, happy endings, at least at that time. Coach Knight went on to a fair amount of success at Texas Tech, where red sweaters were very much in fashion. And Coach Davis rebuilt the Indiana Hoosiers team, leading them to the NCAA Championship game. He was rewarded with a six-year contract as head coach.

Two different people, two different decisions, neither right nor wrong. A yes-you yes-now leader thinks about their loyalties and makes clear decisions based on them. Know what your beacon is and stick to it.

Great Followers Achieve Great Success

"Success is peace of mind which is a direct result of self-satisfaction in knowing you did your best to become the best that you are capable of becoming."[5]

—John Wooden, legendary coach and teacher

The skills and habits needed to be a great follower are key ingredients of a yes-you yes-now leader. If you go back to the table of contents of this book, you can scan down the chapter titles and see a few things.

First, the concepts cover a lot of ground. There is no simple recipe for being a yes-you yes-now leader, but it is not complicated either. By shaping your views from personal experience, you can distinguish yourself in ways that are uniquely yours.

Second, the whole has a greater effect than one or even a few of the concepts on their own. By combining basic concepts, as in the chapter "Do Your Job Well," with other tenets, such as in "Self-Control," you get the benefits of synergy.

Third, the puzzle of putting all the concepts together and practicing them is a challenge that can be done only occasionally at best, perhaps never consistently. To master these concepts is a great accomplishment. When these concepts are linked to the goals of a group, great success can be achieved.

John Wooden was men's basketball coach at UCLA during a period when the UCLA Bruins won 10 NCAA championships. No other team has come close to that performance. That very visible basketball accomplishment made Coach Wooden famous, but he has actually contributed much more to people inside and outside of the world of sports.

In fact, his contributions have been many and great; so great that he was awarded the United States Presidential Medal of Freedom by President George W. Bush in 2003. When presenting the medal, President Bush cited Wooden's teaching about the benefits "of hard work and discipline, patience and teamwork."[6]

Coach Wooden *was* primarily a teacher, whether of English in the classroom or of basketball in the gym. Some of his insights as a teacher started as early as when he was in high school in Indiana during the 1920's. He noticed that students earned grades that didn't always correspond to their effort. He saw some work mightily to earn a C grade, which was met with disappointment by them and others. It was then that young John coined the phrase that opens this chapter and became the basis of his Pyramid of Success.[7]

The phrase is so simple. Do your best to become your best, and you will have peace of mind. Measure yourself against yourself. Others will measure you against others or against standards over which you have no control. All you can do is your best within yourself.

Most of Coach Wooden's players were able to do this. There were players at UCLA who became famous during the years they were there, those who became famous later as professional players in the National Basketball Association, and those who became famous after their playing days were over. Some of the names rekindle the memories of basketball greatness – Kareem Abdul-Jabbar, Bill Walton, Henry Bibby, Walt Hazzard, and Marques Johnson are just a few.

Each of them was a follower of Coach Wooden's simple principle of success, and by acting on that principle they achieved success on and off the court.

But these people, famous or not, knew their success was not based on fame, but on accomplishment. Even those who did not become famous did become successful using the definition they adopted from Coach Wooden. And they've woven this definition into their lives, even passing the concepts on to their children.

Bill Walton's son, Adam, has said of Wooden, "I know every one of his quotes by heart. The Pyramid of Success was plastered on all our walls and still is." Sven Nater taught the principles to his daughters, Alisha and Valerie, while Nater himself became a director at Costco, the national warehouse merchandiser. I saw Valerie play basketball at Enumclaw (Washington) High School and could see the strong work ethic in her play. Mike Warren, who turned down a chance to play in the NBA to pursue acting and became well known as a regular on television's *Hill Street Blues,* did the same for his son, Cash.

They achieved great success by being great followers while practicing yes-you yes-now leadership. They contributed to causes much bigger than themselves, and mastered the diverse skills and practices needed to reach team goals.

Be Pleasant

"While you can't control what happens to you, you can control how you react. Make good manners an automatic reaction."[8]

—John Wooden, legendary coach and teacher

This sounds like something your mother told you years ago! We all know it still holds true but can be darn hard to do all the time.

Being pleasant is a quality people like in both a follower and a leader. Why do we like it? Most would say it is because it makes the teamwork more enjoyable and less stressful, which is undoubtedly true.

Taken another step though, if you are truly enjoying the work and aren't stressed out about it, you and the team will be better able to focus on achieving your goals. Time and energy spent in conflict and conflict resolution are time taken away from the tasks. Being pleasant and being self-aware about it will allow each person to help one another.

Yes-you yes-now leadership can be trying at times, testing your ability to balance conflicting demands. When you feel team pressures, remember they are professional pressures, not personal. Teamwork is most effective when people feel positive about each other and feel that each person is doing their best to meet team objectives. Even when times are tough, be pleasant. Tough problems are hard enough without adding the extra layer of bad behavior.

Being pleasant creates a sense of interdependence and belief that teammates can trust each other. In such a setting, yes-you yes-now leaders put a lot of effort into solving problems and focusing on their own and their teammates' success. Team success will naturally follow.

The trust and positive focus will happen spontaneously if you are lucky enough to be working with mature team-oriented people but this is not likely. So the team must be prepared to spend time and effort to consciously build the culture reinforcing the personal and team value of being pleasant. Conflict can be resolved productively as in the chapter "A Path to Good Group Decisions."

❧

I once worked with a very talented woman whom I will call Jane. She had an unusual ability to listen to people and get the gist of the situation quickly. She was leading a large project so this skill helped her and her teammates identify the inevitable problems large projects have.

In the early stages of the project, people would flock to her, giving her updates and sharing problems. She quickly assessed their information, decided what to do, and dispatched them. It worked well – for a while.

As the work continued, the problems mounted. There were an unusual number of problems, but not only with the project work. The intra-team problems were increasing with no effective means to resolve so many so fast. The problems started to pile up. Eventually, one more problem broke the proverbial camel's back. Chaos ensued.

Jane could no longer deal with so many problems herself and had no strong followers to turn to for help. She continued to bear the burden but the volume was overwhelming and her behavior changed. She snapped at people saying, "If they bring me one more problem, I'll strangle them." When something broke, she went after a person, usually the nearest person, and threatened to fire them. She screamed at them. She swore at them. Her teammates withdrew.

No one wanted that type of treatment, so they started withholding bad news. Jane thought the project had turned itself around, for she was no longer dealing with so much trouble. She had no idea it was actually getting worse because no one wanted to face her unpleasant behavior.

People started to focus on Jane's behavior as the problem, instead of focusing on project problems. The energy of the team was being misdirected to interpersonal conflict rather than being used on work productive for the project. Nothing was getting done. Eventually, the project failed.

For a simple comparison, go watch a youth sports game. When the game isn't going the way a team wants it to go, watch how the team members, both players and coaches, respond. Some start yelling negative things; slam towels or equipment to the ground; or blame others, especially game officials. During a high school basketball game in Seattle, a struggling team's head coach began complaining to the referees about their calls. Within seconds, the players were also complaining, followed shortly thereafter by fans using foul language, mostly adults and many of them parents of the players.

In another game I watched, people shouted encouragement, flashed uplifting smiles, and players ran as hard as they could. While the coach was shouting helpful instructions, the players encouraged each other to higher performance, lifting each other up. Yes-you yes-now behaviors had the most impact!

In each case, you can see how the players, coaches, and fans behaved. So many times, when a team under negative influence disintegrates, it not only loses the game but the players feel terrible about their performance. Teams under pleasant influence rise to the occasion, with no guarantee of victory on the scoreboard. But they always go home feeling good about themselves.

Pleasant behavior is contagious. Or should I say, behavior is contagious. Any member of a team can start the ball rolling either way and a yes-you yes-now leader can set the example.

It's Fundamental

"I'm not looking for a foreign policy expert. I'm looking for someone who knows how to make things work, who can impose order and procedure on the National Security Council."[9]

—Frank Carlucci, National Security Advisor under President Ronald Reagan, when recruiting his leadership team

Effective yes-you yes-now leadership always focuses on solid execution of the fundamentals. Any number of fancy embellishments can't compensate for poor basics and sloppy execution. Every profession and every hobby has its fundamentals. Make sure you know them, practice them, and execute them consistently in support of your personal and team goals.

Your personal habits are also fundamental to your performance. Think twice before you do anything in your private life that would harm your livelihood or your team. Always do productive things to achieve your goals: be courteous, return phone calls, offer to help, and, above all, know how to do your job and do it well.

There was a period in history when men's professional basketball in the United States was falling apart. You might expect this would have been in the early days of the sport or in the early

days of the league. But no, it was actually during the late 1990s and early 21st century when economies were doing well and sports in general were prospering.

But U.S. pro basketball was different than other sports, both on and off the court. Every part of the league seemed to ignore the fundamentals, both on and off the court.

Players lacked good fundamentals in their personal habits. On their personal time, stars had run-in after run-in with the police. They abused drugs, cars, and girlfriends, and were involved with car wrecks, sometimes involving alcohol. Players with multi-million dollar contracts underperformed, distracted by vices. Some stars were rumored to have a child in every city. The Portland Trailblazers picked up the unflattering nickname, "the Portland Jailblazers."

The Portland team was particularly interesting because team management thought fans wanted only a winner and took risks by building a team full of bad attitudes. Only later they found out that the fans really wanted both decent behavior and great basketball. They wanted the San Antonio Spurs, who won NBA Championships *and* were a team of good citizens you could have invited home to your family's dinner table. The Spurs were both well-behaved and were a true team that won championships.

When Starbucks founder Howard Schultz was owner of the Seattle Supersonics, he worked to build a strong community base for his team. He lamented how hard it was to find players with fundamentals in good behavior. A person to fill the dual role of good citizen and good ballplayer was becoming rare.

On the court, the game had eroded to the point of being totally uninteresting. Pass the ball to the big guy near the basket, if he can't shoot cleanly, he would pass it back out to a small guy for a 3-point shot. Back and forth, back and forth. Very little else happened on the court and it wasn't much of a game to watch. John Wooden, the legendary coach whose UCLA teams won 10 NCAA Championships, commented that he much preferred watching women's college and professional basketball because they played with solid execution of the fundamentals of passing, dribbling, running plays, shooting, and rebounding. These skills showed up in a fast-paced game with a variety of offensive plays, in stark contrast to the back and forth passing in men's professional basketball.

And if you did steel your will to watch a pro men's game, you saw highly paid stars breaking fundamental rules over and over. Like traveling with the ball – why so sloppy? Even worse, officials letting them get away with it – why so lax? And the worst, stars complained when it did get called – why so whiny?

The American men's basketball team had completely dominated Olympic basketball for years. The 2004 Olympics saw a much weaker U.S. team performance. Some players complained about international rules and many others complained the U.S. had not brought their "A" team full of professional stars.

But they'd brought together a solid crew of pro players and found that they were still missing the fundamentals after years of NBA play. They were terrible on defense, not helping each other enough, not moving properly on offense, not working around defenders well, and not moving their feet fast enough to stay with their man. They did not have the fundamentals and were beaten by teams that did. After years and years of gold medal performances, in the 2004 Olympic Games, the best they could do was win the bronze medal. Yes-you yes-now leadership was conspicuously absent.

Active Engagement

"I remember meeting these guys and the first thing they said was, 'Let's go to the gym.' When you hear that, you know you're with guys who want to win."[10]

—Al Horford, power forward of the 2006 NCAA College
Basketball Champion Florida Gators

Active engagement is essential by all members of an effective team. Formal leaders are usually actively engaged because they are automatically on the spot. All eyes are focused on what the leader says and does, creating demands to be engaged and respond.

For a follower, active engagement is not demanded because often no one is talking directly to you. It is easy to drift off and disengage. A yes-you yes-now leader has to make a special effort to stay engaged and focused, contributing where appropriate and understanding the dialogue as it unfolds.

I worked as a formal leader on a team of about 200 people. Our job was to provide information systems for a number of major medical centers. These were not ordinary business systems counting the number of widgets or the dollars of revenue earned. These were key clinical information systems that provided data for direct patient care, with safety and lives at stake.

This team had existed for many, many years and people had become quite comfortable in their jobs. Healthcare in general had existed in the lazy backwaters of technology, with little use of computers and no organization demand for them. For years, much patient data was on paper. The reliability of the few systems that were being used was not considered critical by the caregivers that used them nor the administrators controlling the money.

Then in 1999, the Institute of Medicine (IOM) issued a report that said, in part, a lot of patients were dying due to the American health care system; more than from AIDS, breast cancer, or automobile collisions. A number of large companies (who pay for medical coverage of their employees) formed a group called Leapfrog that encouraged the use of more capable information systems in health care as a way of reducing errors. As an example, online records of medications could warn that a newly prescribed drug would have adverse consequences with a drug administered a few hours before.

While the healthcare industry had been the historical laggard regarding systems investments, new external forces were now pushing for improvements. Where I worked, these improvements were to be implemented by our team of people, many of whom had been hired in a different era with very different computing demands.

It was quite evident that the IOM and Leapfrog reports called for change. Our people seemed to intellectually acknowledge that but didn't jump to action.

Our formal leaders held monthly meetings with managers to discuss, engage, and encourage their active engagement to make progress. In the beginning, a different manager hosted these meetings every quarter. That manager created the agendas, arranged for speakers, and led the meetings. Most people avoided this leadership role and joked about who would get stuck with the next quarter's responsibility.

That didn't work. So I tried to focus on topics to move us forward, to really get the group of managers engaged and enthusiastic about the needed changes. It worked for a while, but soon the meeting became one people felt they were forced to attend, waiting passively to see if anything good would happen. Members took absolutely no responsibility for contributing to making something good happen. They just sat there and waited to be entertained. They became negative and critical about another wasted meeting and I considered it a disappointing failure in my leadership.

Then my boss read the book *Good to Great* and wanted to use that as a source for our change efforts. I thought the book was well-written and well-researched; full of stuff to emulate and inspire.

We started to have the monthly meetings with a chapter of *Good to Great* as a discussion focus. The reaction of the team was the same as the previous two versions of the monthly meeting. Flat. Passive. The I'm-not-gonna-speak-up awkwardness we've probably all seen.

There is no happy ending to this story because there was no enthusiasm on the topic. It certainly pointed out what happens when a team is not actively engaged – very little, even with something as important as healthcare at stake. Had a few followers stepped up and exhibited yes-you yes-now leadership, the others might have, too. Take that step towards active engagement for your team and the enthusiasm will propel you forward.

Accentuate the Positive

"Delete the negative; accentuate the positive!"[11]

—Donna Karan, fashion designer

Research has shown that the hurt from loss impacts people more than the pleasure from gain. Speculation abounds as to why this happens. The leading idea is that it's based on a survival instinct. Imagine being out in the forest and a grizzly startles you. You may lose your life if you don't react appropriately. Fear, and the vivid memory of that fear, might keep you from being eaten alive the next time you meet up with a bear. That bad feeling keeps you alive!

Contrast that with an experience that feels good but isn't a matter of life or death, like enjoying a delicious dish of ice cream. You remember the richness of the smooth flavor as a good feeling, but not with the same intensity you felt when you met the grizzly.

With bad feelings dominating our thinking, it would be easy for negative thoughts to slow progress towards team goals. A follower must compensate by making extra effort to accentuate the positive. It is a bit more involved than just making the same number of good and bad things happen, as shown in the following examples.

~~~

Imagine your mind is a marketplace where each bad thing takes $50 from your Mood Account. You start out your day and before you get out the door, something bad happens: you notice a very visible stain on your clothes and it's too late to change them. Subtract $50 from your Mood Account.

Unfortunately good things are only valued at $10 apiece, so you'll need five good things to balance out one bad thing. You get in your car knowing you need to stop for gas, look at the gauge, and to your pleasant surprise see your spouse filled it up for you last night. Add $10 to your Mood Account! You are feeling a bit better now but because the feeling of bad persists, you need the good things to trickle in over time. As the day goes on your Mood Account balance fluctuates: subtract when bad happens, add when good happens.

But wait! Is that all there is to it? Not only is there accounting to be done, there is classifying. The stain on your clothes and the gas in the tank are external events that you classify before your Mood Account is adjusted. The events of the day are what they are. How you interpret them is the key to the balance in your account.

The Massachusetts Institute of Technology is famous for breakthroughs in science and engineering. Thirty-one members of the MIT faculty have received the National Medal of Science and there have been 80 Guggenheim Fellows, 6 Fulbright Scholars, 20 MacArthur Fellows, and 62 Nobel Prize winners. MIT researchers even took us to the moon by developing the flight guidance system for the Apollo lunar missions.[12] Their tremendous success does not come as easily as it may seem.

They achieve great things with great effort that goes unnoticed by the media and casual observer. That effort is to generate the positive outlook to overcome dead-ends and roadblocks that come during a research project. It all looks neat and tidy when presented on the news or written up in a magazine article but the reality is messy.

My son learned this firsthand. He graduated from the University of Colorado and was destined for Navy pilot training in Pensacola, Florida, when he was asked if he was interested in going to graduate school first. He said yes and a few months later found himself in Cambridge, Massachusetts, enrolled in MIT's Department of Aeronautics and Astronautics. It turned out to be as rigorous as expected.

His first year there was filled with ups and downs. He viewed each obstacle as a learning opportunity, whether it was schoolwork or getting money for computers from the professors. It was all a chance to learn.

Late in the school year, his positive thinking was put to a severe test when a series of things happened. He had not done well on an oral math exam. The research computers were too slow and unstable for the team of graduate students. It was taking days to get results for his simulation of jet engine performance. He was feeling low so he called me and we talked through the problems. But more importantly, we talked about how to continue to make progress.

He had some ideas and so did I, suggesting that while he was a follower of the professors, he could nonetheless take concrete action for positive change. We thought there must be a way to find faster computers to use, either from the Navy, another lab at MIT, or from his uncle in the oil business.

He called a meeting of graduate students and faculty to work on the computer problems, explaining how everyone would benefit from improvements. At first no one said anything, all waiting to see who would break the silence. Finally one professor said, "He is making some good points. We should listen." The other professors began to listen and nod their heads in agreement. The bad computer situation was recognized as an opportunity to make things better.

My son, the yes-you yes-now leader, had identified a bad situation that was hurting the entire team of graduate students, classified it as an opportunity for good, and took action for progress. He, a Navy officer, ended up getting access to a faster computer – from the Air Force!

Internal classifying and accounting of events to make them productive and positive doesn't happen naturally for most people. We have to work at it by viewing the events from many different perspectives, which can be hard. Conscious reinforcement of the good things will help keep proper focus, and positive habits will form.

Positive thinking is a technique to master, one so well known that Johnny Mercer and Harold Arlen wrote a song about it in 1944. It was nominated for the 1945 Academy Award for Best Song in the film *Here Come the Waves*. Even if you don't know the tune, the lyrics are worth reading and applying to your role as an effective yes-you yes-now leader.

> You've got to accentuate the positive
> Eliminate the negative
> Latch on to the affirmative
> Don't mess with Mister In-Between

Good news and bad news can be found in any situation and you can be certain to find either if you set your mind on it. Johnny Mercer's lyrics put the responsibility right where it should be. It's the same place Norman Vincent Peale put it in his classic book *The Power of Positive Thinking*. Squarely on you and me.

Power Distribution

People in a group share power. It resides within members of a team and shifts around constantly. It's not just about power though, but also about shifts in power to help focus on the goals of the group.

With a strong central leader, power is concentrated and people are given instructions on what to do and how to do it. Those instructions allow almost no distribution of power from the leader to the followers. It can also lead to a speedy decision that may or may not be well-informed.

The other end of the spectrum is a group where the people decide everything. This means power is decentralized and a slow time-consuming process is needed to make decisions. It doesn't *have* to be slow, of course, but it almost always is, in order to accommodate everyone's opinion.

The first extreme is dangerous because it relies on an all-knowing central figure – which doesn't really exist – although some leaders think they are all-knowing. It also means followers are at risk for their jobs, their promotions, a spot in the starting line-up, or whatever is at stake if they do not do what they are told. Because of that risk, some followers will say yes to whatever the leader says. Even with a mask of kindness, this type of leader rules in fear.

The other extreme is also dangerous because it is difficult for anything to get done. Rules and process help, but too many voices can become unworkable. The group as a whole suffers under its own inability to make decisions and achieve its goals.

❧

History has plenty of examples of the misguided omnipotent formal leader – Hitler, Stalin, Mussolini, and Saddam Hussein are ready examples. They are obvious and extreme cases, but worthy of note because they serve as examples from which to learn. In their stories lie general themes that apply to more commonplace situations that we all encounter in our lives

You don't need to read a lot of history to know about these types of leaders and what they do to their followers. You can probably name a boss of yours, current or former, who believed they were omnipotent. They used their formal position to make the rules, shutting off ideas from other people, and wielding their power like a club.

I had a boss like that. Let's call him Matthew Peterson. He was friendly at first meeting but had an uneasy air that I quickly picked up. It came from him always trying to figure out angles to work in order to give his directives. Other people could see this easily, but not Matthew. He thought he was being clever.

When he gave his directives, he expected people to hop to it. Weak followers did just that. They said it was their job to make their boss look good. I thought that you should actually *do* good work, which would naturally make you and your boss look good – but only as a by-product of the real thing.

Matthew's style was to have a bunch of yes-people working for him. Those who challenged him were quickly on his bad side and their days were numbered. The remaining group of followers lived in fear for their jobs, not in service to their customers. The wrong things were getting done because the focus was not on doing the best thing needed, but merely reacting to the boss.

It made it even harder when he withheld information that his team needed to get their jobs done, even going so far as not telling his team about a new product launch that would need support. Visualize an army of drones from a Star Wars movie, marching forward relentlessly with no knowledge of what they are fighting for. If Matthew Peterson had moved toward a less authoritarian approach, his team could have accomplished their goals more easily and enjoyably.

At the opposite extreme are followers so independent that nothing gets done. Their efforts are disjointed, there is no focus to their cause, and no semblance of leadership for the followers to support.

This is easy to spot if you see a group in which the people don't get anything done. They like to meet and talk because they like to meet and talk. Goal orientation toward a common purpose is a foreign concept. This is often seen in situations where there may be no clear right or wrong, or where there is agreement on "what" needs to happen, but not on the "how" of making it happen.

Civic issues in Seattle and the Puget Sound region of the United States fall into this disorganized mass of followers.

As with many cities around the world, increasing air travel showed that the Seattle-Tacoma International Airport could not sustain the projected volume. New runways or new airports were needed to serve the region. Those facts were clear.

But then came the arguments about what to build and where. The not-in-my-back-yard (NIMBY) syndrome arose front and center. An existing airfield north of Seattle, Paine Field, was underutilized. Why not use it? Because the NIMBY people living around it or under potential flight paths did not want the increased air traffic with its congestion and noise pollution.

A new regional airport east of Seattle was offered as an alternative. Its runways would be built on a ridge to minimize the winter delays when fog often lay in the surrounding valleys. It was a sparsely populated area so noise would not be a major problem.

Or would it? The NIMBY people who lived there said they moved out there to get away from city noise. They wanted no airplanes and no airport. Anyway, who thought it would be a good idea to cut down all the trees and pour concrete?

So the regional committee came right back to Sea-Tac Airport and said, "Let's build another runway there." It seemed to be the idea with least impact, plus the freeways to get there already existed. A lot of money could be saved.

But a third group of NIMBY people popped up and filed a lawsuit to stop the new runway. Challenge after challenge dragged the whole thing out for years.

The people charged with solving the airport problem seemed to have no clear goals and no focus. They got nothing done. If just one yes-you yes-now leader had stepped forward, a resolution meeting the needs of most people could have happened.

Somewhere in between these two extremes is a good balance of follower-leader power distribution. It is not the same for every situation and doesn't remain the same for the duration of a task. It is fluid, but you know you have the right formula if the team is making healthy progress towards its goals without living in fear.

Leading Yourself

A Sense of Duty

"I long to accomplish some great and noble task, but it is my chief duty to accomplish small tasks as if they were great and noble."[14]

—Helen Keller, author and social activist

Duty is remarkable because it makes you do things you never thought you could do. That may sound odd at first because we usually think that incredible feats come from incredible drive, from incredible risk-taking, or from heroics.

Some people choose what they do purely on emotion, by what they feel like doing or not doing. Others make it a fairly analytical process. Choices about what to do next lead to an evaluation of the effort and resources needed, then a comparison to the expected benefits.

Duty, however, can help us do incredible things not because we want to, but because we have to. It arises from a sense of obligation that we must act in certain ways, in accordance with customs and expectations. These can be our own, such as trying to rescue someone from a burning house. Or they can belong to others, such as going to an event because people expect you to be there, not because you want to. In either case there may be payoff, such as saving a life or having a good time meeting new friends and business contacts.

Recognizing the role of duty in your life helps you lead from where you are. You will do things to help your leader and team achieve their goals because you must. This enables you to overcome your personal resistance to doing simple tasks or going the extra mile.

❧

David Rockefeller led a most extraordinary life. It would be easy to assume that much of it was due to being a Rockefeller and that anyone born into that family would have opportunities galore.

That is partly true. In his college years he met many influential people who opened doors for him, such as the time he was staying with family friends in the United Kingdom. The visit resulted in him being interviewed for a newspaper article by Randolph Churchill, son of Winston Churchill.

Joseph Kennedy was ambassador to the Court of Saint James and entertained often at the American Embassy. It was at one such party that Rockefeller first met a future U.S. President, young John F. Kennedy (who had come to London from Harvard especially for the party).

But much of Rockefeller's experience as a young man was formed by his own choices about where he went and who he met. While in college, he traveled through Europe as any other college student would. While in Germany, he witnessed the funeral procession for General Erich Ludendorff who was a key German leader during World War I. This was 1937 and the parade was filled with SS officers goose-stepping en masse. At the head of the column, surrounded by Nazi salutes and shouts of "Sieg Heil," was Adolf Hitler. Rockefeller was overwhelmed by the excited crowd and uncomfortable with all it represented.

When Pearl Harbor was attacked, Rockefeller talked with a friend of his, Dick Gilder. They had both visited Europe years earlier and had suspected war was inevitable. Gilder had a wife and two children. While he was a dedicated family man, his sense of duty to his country and the principles of freedom made him decide to enlist in the military to fly in Europe.

Knowing that the odds of a pilot returning safely were low, he asked Rockefeller to look after his family should he not return. This was a shock to Rockefeller.

Rockefeller was unsure about his own plans regarding the war. He had married only a year earlier and his wife was pregnant with their first child. Given his privileged upbringing, he was uncertain about how he would cope with the rigors of military service. A family friend could certainly ensure his exemption from the draft. And then he had a conversation with his mother.

Abby Rockefeller had long been a pacifist but the attack on Pearl Harbor had changed her views. She had become seriously concerned about the threat of Hitler to Western civilization. She told David that she now believed that eligible men should do their part by enlisting in the service. It was their duty. She told him, her son, that it was his duty to fight even though he would risk his life doing so.

This conversation persuaded him to enlist in the Army as a private, disregarding the influence of his wealthy father who could have helped him join as an officer. Enlisted or officer, his father's influence might have also kept him in a safe state-side military job, but David chose to follow duty and go overseas.

Rockefeller went through the rigor of Army training and saw duty in Northern Africa and in Europe. In the course of his assignments, he met people who would later become influential in their own right, such as William Paley who started CBS, John Kluge who founded Metromedia, and John Oakes who became an editor at the New York Times.

As an enlisted soldier, Rockefeller was given assignments he would have missed as an officer, allowing him the chance to meet these people and see the war from the grassroots. While he developed into a great leader, his Army experiences as a follower helped instill in him a lifelong sense of duty.

Emotion as a Trigger

"The degree of one's emotions varies inversely with one's knowledge of the facts."[15]

—*Bertrand Russell, logician and philosopher*

Emotions are an essential part of being human. We have them all the time, no effort required. Another part of being human is the ability to make choices, and the responsibility that comes from the impact of those choices. A yes-you yes-now leader knows how to make good choices.

Think about when an emotion is used as a trigger for a decision. You see or hear some information and immediately feel happy or sad. Now use that feeling as the signal that you should do something about it, such as run up to hug and kiss a person who made you happy, or smile and say thanks, or do nothing at the time but go home and write a thank you note. How well you know the person plays into your decision. So does where you are and who you are with. Add your sense of the magnitude of the happy information, and you can quickly see that all of these factors are based on what you think, not on the emotion itself.

Sometimes spontaneous decisions and actions are great. More often in the role of the yes-you yes-now leader, a bit more thought helps you and the team.

Any two people living, working, or playing together are going to have occasional conflict. I say this, you hear that. I leave the lid up, you want it down. You take a screwdriver, I can't find it when I need it. You squeeze the toothpaste tube from the bottom up, I just squeeze it out any old way. These are not big deals in substance, but may get emotionally escalated due to choice or as an indicator of deeper problems.

Because these behaviors can happen between any number of people, the role of the follower is critical – indeed the follower may become the leader and roles may change throughout the course of the conversation.

Each of the preceding examples can cause an emotional reaction. Why did he say that? Why can't she put the tools back? After all these years, doesn't he know that bothers me?

The emotional reaction is what it is. Yes, a person can work to change one's reactions over a period of time, but they are sometimes just normal. After all, when I need a tool from my toolbox I want it to be there. I'm annoyed when it's not. It doesn't matter whether I was the last one to use it or someone else was. At that moment, I am irritated that I will have to spend 10 minutes finding the tool instead of fixing the doorknob.

Choice comes after the emotional reaction. Where do I want the issue to go? Do I want to get myself so upset that I decide to use the wrong tool and damage the doorknob in the process? Do I want to yell at anyone nearby (spouse, children, neighbor, pet), even though I know they don't have the tool? Do I want to guess who had it last and go yell at them? Shall I just go find it, making a mental note to talk about it later to see if we need to buy an extra tool for someone?

There are many, many choices, which is why the follower role is so important. The person who starts a conversation usually takes the lead. The other people follow, at least for a while, and have immense influence on the course of the conversation. How the follower reacts and responds is critical.

A calm measured response will de-escalate the tension, while an angered response may result in increased irritation and retaliation from the leader.

I was in a work meeting where a director-level person spoke to me with an annoyed tone and anger showing on his face. My response was, "John, I can tell this issue is important to you. I can imagine how frustrating it must feel." Later that day, another person who was in the meeting came to me and said the immediate change in John's body language was obvious. I had de-escalated the tension and turned myself from the follower into the leader, for the moment at least. John then regained his composure and moved on to a productive meeting.

The first choice of action is critical, yet it is amazing how so many people don't get this. They get so caught up in who is right and who is wrong. There is a lot of blaming at this stage because the situation is not good – at least bad enough to have generated an emotional reaction from you.

How does blaming get you any closer to resolution? It doesn't, of course. But blaming is a secondary event. It is one of the choices available to you after the initial emotional reaction. And therefore, you have a choice about whether to blame or not.

Years ago I attended a management seminar in which each participant was given a set of U.S. coins; one each of a dollar, a fifty cent piece, a quarter, a dime, a nickel, and a penny. Each time we encountered a problem in our lives, we were to assign that problem's value to one of the coins. A dollar problem would be a major issue such as the death of a loved one, and the problems scale down from there. By doing this, we quickly realized that most problems that seem huge are really of the one cent and five cents variety.

The power of the coin exercise is to make a choice more obvious – choice about the magnitude of problems to properly guide a set of possible actions to one appropriate for the situation. This is a useful tool for a yes-you yes-now leader to recall during times of conflict and to use to de-escalate the conflict.

Making smart choices defines how you spend your time, how productive you are, how happy you are with your productivity, and the tone of your relationships with your teammates. In a roundabout way, it defines who you really are. Followers are surprised to rationally think through how much choice they have about these things, especially if they have had the habit of simply reacting to life events.

The most surprising and wonderful aspect of making choices is how easy it is to do. Equally surprising is how few times people do it well. Why this paradox? Simply because the easy act of making a choice requires the difficult act of emotional control and discipline to frame the choices. You control your emotions … or your emotions will control you.

Emotions are the source motivation for us to take action. They are good to get us going. But they do not give us much help in deciding which way to go. Emotion and intelligence are partners, one to provide the spark and the other to carry out the mission by choosing actions consistent with the desired goals. An effective yes-you yes-now leader knows how to make these choices.

Being Accountable for Doing Your Job

"It is not only what we do, but also what we do not do, for which we are accountable."[16]

—Moliere, 17th century playwright

When all is said and done, it is you and only you who are accountable for doing your job. Too many people seem to develop the habit of thinking that factors outside of their control give them excuses for poor performance. A yes-you yes-now leader cannot rely on their teammates, formal leader, or external factors to be used as an excuse for not getting the job done.

This doesn't mean nothing ever goes wrong and you always achieve peak performance. In the real world unexpected things happen. In fact, if all of your work looks like 100% all of the time, you probably are *under*-performing what you are capable of doing. You know that better than anyone else. That is where the term "slacker" originated.

Slacker behavior can happen at any time, its onset triggered by a range of factors such as boredom with the work, conflict at work, or major personal life events. In my career, I've seen people's performance go on a roller coaster ride, not just occasionally but as a matter of course. They just didn't seem to have the self-regulation to keep their performance up, resulting in significant impact to their work, their team, their leader, and those very important team goals.

At other times I have seen people who were going through some difficult times and they kept performing. Occasionally I had no knowledge of any personal difficulties until well after the fact. In each situation, performance was consistently high.

One case is particularly notable because it showed the importance of adhering to principles in order to be an effective yes-you yes-now leader.

When my daughter was a recent college graduate, we gave her three months of financial support after the commencement ceremony. She didn't have a career job at graduation, so she had to cobble together the means to support herself once the safety net was removed.

She first got a job at an upscale restaurant and started out at the bottom. She worked hard and advanced quickly, but it wasn't enough work to pay the bills. The restaurant hours were mostly lunch and dinner throughout the week. She searched and searched to find the extra income she needed.

Enter Starbucks. Plenty busy in the morning hours which would fit right in with the lunch/dinner schedule at the restaurant. Nice fit.

Then one day the restaurant manager commented on the number of resumes she had received about a help-wanted ad for a weekend bookkeeper. After the dot-com bust, she was seeing resumes from former CFOs! She confided to Emily that these people had the financial background, but the restaurant had always been more successful hiring people they knew were good workers, smart, and able to learn. She asked Emily if she would be interested in learning to do the weekend books. Emily answered with an emphatic "Yes!" The weekend hours would fit in nicely with her weekday commitments.

Out of the blue, the mother of a former high school basketball teammate called and said she'd heard Emily was back in town with degree in hand. Would she be interested in working at the local bank? Of course she would! It was an entry-level teller job, but an entrée into banking. The pay wasn't great but the experience would build on what she'd learned in the food service industry and would be a great step for a career job.

Within months she had interest from another bank about a job which paid her significantly more. Needing the income to be self-sufficient, she explained the situation to her present employer. They were not able to pay her more and understood her need to grow her career. Off she went to the new banking job.

She knew the job would be a challenge. It was primarily loan sales and she wasn't sure she was well suited for sales. But she took the risk to find out. She hated it. She was worried that she was selling loans to people who might not need them. She cried about her unhappiness every few weeks. She wanted to quit.

But her principles told her that it was her job to do her job. Period. She soon learned that adults are free to make their own choices about whether to take out a loan, no matter how illogical the choice seemed to her.

So she learned the ropes and became very good at producing results. Soon she was selling more loans than people with years of experience. She earned bonuses, something she never thought she could do in that job.

When the time came to move on, she did something even more amazing. The company had a policy that you must be on the payroll on the date bonuses are paid or you don't get the money, keeping that carrot dangling out there. When she laid out her career transition plan to return to college and become a teacher, she realized she would miss out on that quarterly bonus because classes started in just two months.

Isn't this when severe short-timer's attitude (STA) kicks in? Many people get STA when they are going on vacation, with low productivity a week before they go. Most get STA when leaving a job. Hardly anyone would produce more work knowing they wouldn't get paid for it.

Emily was one of those few. In her last month, she produced more than ever. Her district manager took her out to lunch to celebrate her accomplishments. It was stellar performance because Emily has stellar principles. She never saw a bonus. She was simply accountable – to herself – for doing her job.

Flatlined

"Self-acceptance comes from meeting life's challenges vigorously. Don't numb yourself to your trials and difficulties, nor build mental walls to exclude pain from your life. You will find peace not by trying to escape your problems, but by confronting them courageously. You will find peace not in denial, but in victory."[17]

—J. Donald Walters, author and composer

Yes-you yes-now leaders must realize that confronting a difficult challenge is the only way to grow and improve. Running away from the challenge is the worst thing you can do. Nearly as bad from a personal and team point of view is staying within your comfort zone, to take on only what you have mastered and what you know to be well within your capabilities. This is the status quo, the steady state. You are flatlined.

൞

I once worked with a woman who was very capable but consistently underestimated her ability. Consequently she limited herself when she had the personal choice of taking on new challenges, staying within her comfort zone. Her development was slowed because of this and in some areas she did not develop at all.

What is most interesting about this woman is that she could have done almost anything that needed to be done, in the classic style of a complete team player. She was college-educated and had a strong work ethic. She had taken that foundation and developed incredible strengths in people leadership.

When asked, she effectively led project development teams, and established and managed customer support teams including one that was very large scale serving thousands of people.

But the key to the great things she accomplished was that she was asked to take on those tasks. She did not stretch herself to seek opportunities of her own choice. In fact, when aware of the potential of doing new tasks but not being asked or told to do them, she would not take the initiative to pursue them.

If I pointed out that the opportunity was there, she would say "You know I'm not good at that."

Well, of course she wasn't *already* good at that, she had never done it before. But she had the capability of doing it and was choosing to remain in her comfort zone, to the exclusion of her own development. And most incredibly, although she wasn't yet good at the task, she often was the most qualified of *any* person in the company.

She chose to avoid the difficult challenge, chose to avoid what the team needed. She chose to pass over opportunities to help the team achieve its goals. In one particularly important case, the team needed someone to create the outline of a project plan to replace old computer network gear with new models. This clearly had a technical component and required interacting with network gear manufacturers to pick the correct machines.

But this was really a people and task management project. Get the right people together, figure out the team objectives, define criteria, define alternatives, select preferred alternative, then go buy and install the computers. The technical part of the work could be handled by the "right people" while she could have led the process. Unfortunately she declined, deferring to someone with more technical expertise – who also had no time for another project. That project was put on hold, a ripple effect of one person staying within her comfort zone. She was flatlined.

The cost of the ripple effects throughout many projects was significant, both in dollars and team morale. Projects were delayed and people watched a teammate letting them down. The flatlining continued until the person finally left the organization.

Yes-you yes-now leaders know that they must take the initiative for their own growth. It is most productive to grow doing something you like and something the team needs. This contributes much to making progress toward the goals of the group. Imagine having a full team of people who continually accept challenges for their own improvement by taking on difficult tasks for the good of the team. Be one of those people.

Headstrong

"And other people are so stubborn! Possibly unlike you, I actually get paid to try to convince people that I am right and they are wrong, and thank goodness I'm not paid on the basis of results."[18]

—Michael Kinsley, journalist and commentator

There are times when the follower thinks he or she is the leader, when actually someone else is in the leader role. Who decides?

If there is a clear formal power hierarchy, someone will give in. Usually the follower, trying to claim the leadership role, is the one who gives. This can be particularly vexing when the formal hierarchy for leadership power conflicts with the power base arising from having subject-matter expertise. The leader is the boss on paper; the follower knows more about the actual work that is being done. It may take a bit of negotiation, verbal or non-verbal, to break the stalemate. Sometimes the initial disagreement is handled quickly, but the underlying problem remains for a long time. As the following example shows, a headstrong follower in the wrong situation can have severe repercussions.

In the early 1960s, President John F. Kennedy announced the intention of the United States to put a man on the moon and return safely to Earth before the end of the decade. The Americans and the Soviets had barely entered the space age when this bold goal of the moon landing was made.

The first rocket ships were the same type of machines used for military warhead launches and they were not 100% successful. The series of manned spaceflights that would lead to a moon landing required pioneering astronauts willing to risk their lives.

Military test pilots were prime candidates. They had the physical fitness, the stamina, the risk-taking desire, and the bold attitudes to get the job done. They were seasoned military men, fully accustomed to the command hierarchy. They knew that disciplined execution of procedures was the route to success unless something went drastically wrong. Then they would do what was necessary to survive.

The space program started with the Mercury flights in which one astronaut flew each mission. These were sub-orbital at first, then became earth orbiting as experience was gained. The Mercury program was followed by Gemini flights with two astronauts on each mission. Next were the Apollo flights which required three astronauts – the ships that would take humans to the moon.

Wally Schirra was one of the early pioneers. He had developed a reputation for being a great flier, but was also a bit surly at times. He had done his job well on the Mercury Sigma 7 flight, followed by similar success on Gemini flights. You had to be tough to do those jobs, packed into a small cramped space and rocketed out of this world. Wally Schirra was tough, as were his fellow astronauts.

When the Apollo program started, Deke Slayton, the man responsible for NASA crew assignment, named Schirra commander of Apollo 2. Knowing Schirra had had a long career, Slayton figured he would retire soon. Apollo 2 would be a good command for Schirra to have a successful career-capping flight, since this mission was to duplicate and verify everything Apollo 1 was to do.

Schirra was unhappy with doing repetitious mission work and let it be known. He vocally complained about having to repeat everything, and that doing so was a waste of a mission. He wanted the NASA leaders to give them something new and interesting to do. Eventually NASA's upper management agreed that it would be unnecessary to duplicate all of Apollo 1 and cancelled Apollo 2. Who was in charge now? It seemed that the follower, Wally Schirra was by getting NASA to agree, but he lost his flight.

There was more to come. Schirra was assigned as commander of Apollo 7. He was on the flight with Donn Eisele and Walt Cunningham. The three of them had a lot of input into the design of their spacecraft and felt very comfortable critiquing everything – not only the ship, but the mission tests they were performing. They complained about everything, including the food. Their behavior became contagious and some of their attitude came out over public radio broadcasts that the astronauts did about the mission.

Schirra called someone a name. Comments were made about dumb tasks. Schirra told Mission Control that they were not going to do any more tests that were just made up. The commander of the spaceship had challenged the authority of the mission command on Earth. All three astronauts refused to follow procedures to wear their helmets for Earth re-entry because they had head colds. This was in direct violation of orders from ground control. It wasn't going to hurt the mission but the attitude was near mutiny. Who was leading and who was following?

Deke Slayton knew what had to be done. None of the three astronauts of Apollo 7 ever flew in space again. Wally Schirra, the only man to have flown in space in all three programs – Mercury, Gemini, and Apollo – was grounded.

Self-Control

"The best time for you to hold your tongue is the time you feel you must say something or bust."[19]

—Josh Billings, author and humorist

There is an often repeated maxim that tells us "Control your emotions, or they will control you." If you are emotionally out of control, and saying and doing things that provide you some indefinable immediate relief, is it really leading to something helpful for your team? Yes-you yes-now leaders hold the goals of the group as their highest interest. They act in ways that make progress toward the goal by influencing teammates with the end in mind. You can never hope to encourage the positive direction of the others if you cannot control yourself.

Wanting to lash out is normal and okay, but actually lashing out is not okay. Are your words and deeds purposeful, beyond your own selfish need to explode? Will blowing up at someone achieve anything? Will you really feel better if you've unloaded but fouled up everything by alienating your team members and taking the team off track?

It is rare, but truly revealing, when a person is emotionally out of control yet recovers quickly to act in a responsible manner.

Once the emotional outburst is unleashed, it is hard for anyone within earshot, whether personally or through the amplifying effect of the media, to forget what just happened. It always looks like a mess.

This is particularly true at work, where there is no official record of who did what or who said what to whom, and just what did they mean by that anyway? So much is hidden behind the closed doors of meeting rooms and offices. People see one part of the issue but not the whole picture. The fragmentation of the whole picture leads people to different conclusions about what is really going on, which leads to a wide range of solutions to essentially different problems. The mess continues.

I once observed a particularly vivid and colorful office meltdown – screaming, profanity, and flailing arms. The human impact of the debacle was so large that word spread to hundreds of people in three buildings within 30 minutes! By the next morning I started hearing the story from other people through the grapevine. All the stories were equally strong about the emotions, but all were equally off-base about the content. No one even had an accurate picture of the issue that caused the meltdown. If the perpetrator had had the sense to realize the impact of her behavior, she would have been embarrassed – I hope.

So it was fascinating when a story of a *potential* emotional outburst showed up in the national press not long ago. How many times do people warn you that they are going to meltdown in a few days?

But the meltdown never happened. And it didn't happen for all the right reasons.

Love him or hate him, George Steinbrenner had owned the New York Yankees baseball team for years. He had been known for being arbitrary, insisting on his own way, acting without explanation, demanding a winning team, and willing to have the highest payroll in baseball to get the talent to win.

So it was not surprising to have a certain amount of controversy when the Yankees won the American League Championship in 2003 and went to the World Series. What was surprising was that one of the controversies involved 72-year-old Don Zimmer, a long-time baseball manager employed for years with the Yankees. Just after winning the American League pennant, Zimmer said he did not know what the future held for him, but he would have something to say about Mr. Steinbrenner after the World Series. The warning of the impending meltdown and it wasn't going to be pretty.

You could sense the dissension in the clubhouse as the week wore on, everyone wondering what Zimmer was going to say and what he would do.

They didn't have to wait long. Shortly after the Florida Marlins beat the Yankees in Game 6 of the Series, Zimmer quietly announced that he was simply quitting his job. Not retiring from baseball, but quitting his job with the Yankees.

This was quite a reversal for someone who had told the media, only a week before, that he was going to unload on George Steinbrenner. What had happened to lead Zimmer to the point of wanting to unload, then not doing it? Many events led up to it, but just one powerful idea stopped him.

Zimmer said he had been friends with Steinbrenner for over 20 years, going to the horse races together many times. The relationship was friendly but had its formal leader-follower order. Zimmer said, "For 25 years, Steinbrenner called me 'Zimmer' and I called him 'Boss.'"

Something changed, causing Steinbrenner to begin a series of slights. The turn of events had started the previous winter, when Zimmer said they ran into each other at a racetrack and Steinbrenner would not talk to him. When spring training started, Zimmer was informed he wouldn't be getting a courtesy car like all the other Yankee coaches. When a regular season giveaway of Don Zimmer Bobblehead Dolls was proposed, Steinbrenner apparently stopped it. There was even a report that Steinbrenner told TV camera crews not to point cameras at Zimmer.

So the powder keg was full and the fuse was in place, only awaiting the end of the season for the match to be struck and to ignite the explosion that had been promised just one week before from a very emotional Don Zimmer.

Then he calmly announced he was quitting. In the news conference he told the story of the 'Boss' and 'Zimmer' names, and said only, "From now on as far as I'm concerned, he's just Steinbrenner." No emotional tirade. No disrespect. No getting even. Why?

As he choked back a few tears, Zimmer said," I woke up this morning and my wife was crying. She said, 'Don't make yourself a little man.'" And he didn't.[20]

Version Control

"Memory is the way we keep telling ourselves our stories – and telling other people a somewhat different version of our stories."[21]

—Alice Munro, short story author

How many times have you heard more than one story recounting the same event and wondered how they could all be so different? One story may seem more believable to you than the others, so do you support that one?

An effective yes-you yes-now leader must be careful about supporting any of them, let alone just one of them. That's commonly known as "taking sides" and generally has unpleasant consequences. It starts a group of people down the path of pointing the finger at who's right and who's wrong, focusing on the people involved instead the events that transpired.

It's more useful to understand that many people viewing the same event *will* have different versions of what happened. That's why we have trials with many witnesses. The role of the judge or jury is to piece together, as best as they can, what really happened from all the different viewpoints given. What's usually true is that no *single* version is correct and the proper blending and balancing of everyone's story is the best way to figure out what really happened.

Suspend your judgment until you hear from everyone. While not always possible, a good effort will get you the best available information and build confidence of fairness within your team.

❧

The simplest example might be a car wreck. Let's say it happened at the intersection of 3rd and Main. You have six witnesses: one on each of the four corners and a person in each of the cars that were following the two that collided.

Physically, their points of view are different.

While one person sees mostly the fronts of two cars, the person on the opposite corner sees only the backs. Those witnesses in line with the direction of travel will have a very different opinion of the speed of the cars than the people viewing from the side. Imagine how altered your perception would be if you were in the path of the two cars!

Now add the witnesses' mental states to the mix. One just got off a 12-hour shift at work; one just awakened a few minutes earlier and is still groggy on their way to get coffee; one had just finished a two–mile run and is alert and energized; and another pedestrian had just nearly been hit in a crosswalk a few blocks away. Think for a moment of the different states of mind of each person.

This divergence of the "truth" tells us that in matters of observation and recollection the human mind is very imprecise and easily influenced by many factors. Post-wreck measurements, such as the length of the skid marks, will give some of the facts.

From that data, the speed might be calculated. Even that fact might be disputed by a witness in any of the preceding physical locations or states of mind.

More complex situations get even more interesting. In the 2004 U.S. presidential campaign there was a tremendous controversy about Democratic candidate John Kerry's military record and uproar over his actions during the Vietnam War. There is clearly political motivation in campaign issues, but this was particularly interesting – some might say silly – because a lot of people were insisting their version of the story was accurate, even though they were recalling events from *35 years prior.*

During the verbal sparring some said Kerry pursued a "young Viet Cong in a loincloth" while others said it was "a grown man, dressed in the kind of garb the VC usually wore." Could there have been two people? Differences in lighting? Trees or shrubs obscuring someone's vision?

The passage of time is a great modifier of our memories, no matter what our point of view or emotional state may have been when the actual events occurred. At a certain point, you may realize there is no truth to be found. It no longer exists, and a single truth may have never existed.

The yes-you yes-now leader asks about the intended goal of pursuing the controversy, then proposes more productive ways to achieve that goal. Multiple versions of events will always exist. Arguing about who is right will always be destructive. Establishing a desired outcome and working together towards it builds strong, effective teams.

Wrestling with Temptation

"I don't understand myself sometimes. I always try to do what I know to be right but I do not do it. Instead, I do the very thing I should not."[22]

—St. Paul, reflecting on himself around the year 55 A.D.

People have wrestled with temptation forever but there seems to be no cure. Many do what they want to do rather than what they know they must do. The challenge to the yes-you yes-now leader is to resist the temptation to do what they want to do and to channel all of their thoughts and energy towards the goals of the group, in support of their teammates and team goals.

This is a challenge because the goals of everyone are not always perfectly aligned. The concept of entropy says that without an input of energy, things tend to fall apart. You have to spend time, energy, or money to keep a team in top shape. Overcoming temptation takes effort and focus.

It was about two thousand years ago when St. Paul said he didn't understand himself. There is a hint of self-disapproval in his words that each of us has felt. No surprise. Overall, greater happiness has been linked with the strong self-discipline a person needs to do the right thing. A study at Stanford University shed some light on the matter.

In the research study, preschoolers were given a choice between eating one marshmallow immediately or waiting fifteen minutes and eating two marshmallows. Naturally some jumped at the first one and promptly ate it.

Others chose to wait and distracted themselves by napping, covering their eyes, or singing loudly. Then they got their double reward. Ten years later the researchers located these children and administered additional testing and observation. They found that those who had waited for two marshmallows tested as being both smarter and more self-confident![23]

The odd thing about self-control, and indeed all forms of personal discipline, is that it seems constraining and limiting. After all, you're telling me I can't do what I want to do. But psychologists tell us differently. Self-control frees us from being slaves to our temporary impulsive desires, allowing us to behave in line with our deepest beliefs and most important goals, thus improving our overall success.

Contrast this with modern Western culture, where shallow marketing-driven pop culture bombards us with messages appealing to temporary impulsive desires. This isn't just an ideological issue. It leads to underachievement, buying too much on credit, reduced investing for the future, and health problems – more than half of all Americans are now overweight.

With repeated messages about instant gratification we become conditioned to expecting it. Then we run into the team sport, the work project, or the family issue that involves real people and real problems to solve. They defy quick fixes, requiring a conscious effort to have the willpower to overcome the temptation of doing whatever you feel like. It is not about you, it is about your commitment to your team or your family.

Some people simply give up. If there's no quick fix, they don't have the willpower to do what they know they should do. Beyond how they feel, there are reasons why this is true. Willpower can weaken the longer you need to use it. That's why reinforcing and supporting your friends, family, teammates, and leaders is so important.

A study at Florida State University[24] showed the gradual erosion of willpower over time by assembling two groups of very hungry college students and giving them each a plate of chocolate chip cookies and a plate of radishes.

One group was told to eat all the cookies while the other was told to be strong and eat only the radishes. Then the people in both groups were all instructed to perform a tedious task for as long as they could. The students who had spent mental energy making themselves eat radishes gave up on the tedious task long before the chocolate chip cookie eaters. The inference from this study is that if you are faced with a lot of temptations, it may become more and more difficult to resist, unless you use some techniques to overcome them.

Two of the most successful techniques are worth mentioning. One is to anticipate temptations before they come up and make plans to deal with them. The degree of mental preparation prior to facing temptation seems to make it easier to resist and maintain resistance. So prepare yourself when you know you'll be driving by that donut store.

The other is to figure out your personal high risk situations, those in which you know you will likely be tempted, such as moods, time of day, stage of life, locations, weather patterns, and so on. You can prepare yourself for these situations or just avoid them altogether.

While these ideas and techniques may not be a cure for the weakness of willpower, they will help you and your team achieve your goals by helping each other resist the temptation to quit.

A software development project team faced that situation one Saturday evening. They had worked long and hard all week but hadn't yet reached their goal for the week. Their boss saw the energy of the team dropping and heard a few people say they'd rather be home with their families.

The boss decided it would be best to tell the team to go get some rest and come back on Monday ready to go. She assembled the team in the meeting room, thanked them for their work, and suggested they all wrap up and leave.

One software developer didn't like that idea and said so. She said while moods were poor and people were tired and hungry, she thought it would be better for her, and perhaps others, if they rallied together for one last push to finish the week's work – then go home. At first people looked at her like she was crazy. Then one person spoke up in agreement, followed by more. Within a minute the team had decided to stay and finish.

Tempted with going home, one yes-you yes-now leader wrestled the entire team – and their boss – away from the temptation to quit before they had reached their goal.

Making Choices

"When your values are clear to you, making decisions becomes easier."[25]

—Roy E. Disney, Walt Disney Company legend and nephew of Walt Disney

We all know it's important to have a sense of how your teammates and leaders think. We see the beauty of a no-look pass in basketball or a musician who spontaneously and smoothly skips a note to compensate for another musician who got off beat. Some of these behaviors are developed through years of working together. Yet there is one key characteristic you can pick up on quickly – how your teammates make choices. Surprisingly, such simple insight has far-reaching impact because as you begin to anticipate their choices, you adapt your choices to get higher performance, for both the individual and the team.

As the number of choices we face has increased, so has research to help us understand the impact on us of all these choices. With no choice, people have deep negative emotion. Give us a few choices and we're pretty happy. But give us too many choices and we react negatively, not only to the choices, but also with our overall attitude.[26]

When researching people's reactions to choices, two distinct profiles emerge. One attempts to maximize every decision. The other makes "good enough" decisions. Of course there are variations in behavior between these two extremes, but the tendencies are clear: maximizers spend a lot of time and energy making decisions. They are often less satisfied with good results; worse yet, they are more unhappy with bad results.

On the other hand, the good-enough decision-makers don't worry if they later find something better. No surprise, they seldom do because they quit looking once they make a decision. They are happier overall and they approach situations with a positive outlook.

This has shown up in data indicating that over the past thirty years in the United States, as the number of choices has increased, the proportion of the population describing themselves as very happy has decreased five percent – 14 million people. That same trend can show up within your team.

❧

In April 2004, Scientific American magazine published an article about the "tyranny of choice" in which author Barry Schwartz cited research saying too many choices makes for misery. He describes maximizers as people who try to get the most out of their decisions, even small ones like picking out a movie at the video store or television channel surfing to find the best thing to watch.

There are a few things maximizers do that set them apart. First is how they handle opportunity costs. This simply means that if you decide to do A, you can't do B so you miss out on B.

As obvious as this seems, few people clearly think about it. Maximizers do.

As the number of choices increase, each choice not selected adds to the downside of every decision. If you get one unit of bad feeling by not choosing to have lunch at the Pizzeria, you will likely still enjoy your lunch at Maxie's. But if your decision also weighed the merits of Burgerhouse, Taco Extreme, and The Cloud Room, you get one unit of bad feeling for each of them, and a much deeper sense of lost opportunity costs. Maximizers struggle with this and it affects their disposition and their ability to be happy with the decision. The good-enoughs don't search for the best choice, so they don't accumulate so many units of opportunity costs.

Second, once a decision is made, maximizers dwell on it more, leading to feelings of regret. They think the only way to ensure you will not regret a decision is to make the best possible decision. But that means many choices and lots of analysis, increasing the sense of opportunity cost and the chance that regret will be felt. In a classic test of regret, theater tickets were sold for a series of performances to two groups of people. One group paid full price and the other received a discount. Tracking attendance, researchers found people in the full-price group were more likely to attend in their attempt to minimize the regret of not using a valuable ticket.

Third, as people tend to adapt to new things, we take for granted that new things will be positive. We become irritated by the negative. Enthusiasm about positive experiences does not last very long. We may experience regret about what we did not choose and disappointment with what we did choose. If maximizers carry the burden of trying to make the perfect decision, they will experience the less-than-satisfied feelings of adaptation more strongly.

Finally, maximizers tend to have much higher expectations than good-enough people. Maximizers are therefore very concerned about all of the best-choice, minimize-regrets factors. They will search long and hard, investing more time and effort into obtaining the best.

I've seen this phenomenon in action with an acquaintance who needed a new car. With a purchase of that magnitude, she struggled with opportunity costs. It was very clear that there was only enough money to buy one car. The tradeoffs of so many dimensions such as cost, styling, gas mileage, cargo space, and passenger comfort, created conflict.

She collected data from consumer magazines and car companies. She took test drives and talked with her friends. And in the process of consciously refining what she wanted, she was also subconsciously accumulating opportunity costs.

When she had narrowed her choices down to a few sport utility vehicles, the pressure of lost opportunities exploded. This SUV had huge cargo space with the seat folded down but there was no rear jump seat for two extra passengers like another SUV had. Another could tow a large load but the gas mileage paled compared to all others. The analysis was carried into spreadsheets with scoring of features. Adding them up gave a numerical ranking of the SUVs but did not resolve the nagging feeling of lost opportunities.

About this time, she noticed her family was becoming irritated with the process. They urged her to just go buy something – anything. Spare yourself, and us, the misery. They did not understand that she was a maximizer and they were not. The family had arguments and they were not about the features or specific SUVs, but rather more about the decision-making style.

When she finally made her choice, she drove home with a sense of relief instead of excitement. Her family was just glad to have the process over. She loved the handling, the stereo system, and the visibility she had riding high above the traffic. She felt she had made a good choice.

A few months later all the newness had worn off. She'd now had plenty of experience climbing way up into the driver's seat. She hadn't even thought about that at first, but now it was a real bother, especially during rainy weather when the door jamb was wet and her clothes brushed against it. She recalled how one other SUV had a lower height and a solid step up into the car. Disappointment had set in.

She reassessed her entire method of making the SUV choice and concluded that it was a good process. Overall, she was happy with her car.

But she had not anticipated the family friction during the decision process and was working to help people understand. I took the bold step of offering her the Scientific American article, wondering how she would react. Fortunately, she liked it and used it to share with her family. None of them wanted to adopt her choice process, but they also understood their own style a bit better.

Where people fall on the scale from maximizer to good-enough can impact their ability to be a good follower and support the ability to achieve group goals. The maximizer may get better results, but at what cost? And the good-enough people may be happier and easier to work with, but at what cost? Understanding this about your teammates and leader will help you balance each and improve your ability to lead from where you are.

Breaking the Rules

"I always say that it's about breaking the rules. But the secret of breaking rules in a way that works is understanding what the rules are in the first place."[27]

—Rick Wakeman, innovative musician

Every individual and every group of people establish guidelines and rules to govern their behavior. Without them, we wouldn't function very well, though many times we don't like to operate within their boundaries. Car commercials and song lyrics have encouraged people to color outside of the lines; a fun whimsical urge if you are singing or coloring but potentially dangerous while actually driving a car.

How do you know when to follow the rules or break them? On a team, if too many people were breaking too many rules too much of the time, chaos would rule. What is the right balance?

A yes-you yes-now leader actually has an obligation to challenge the rules and in some cases, to break them. Rules, guidelines, and even laws were written to get the best results most of the time for most of the parties, given the criteria and knowledge present when the rule was made. Do those conditions always apply? Are there times you go against the rule to get to your goal? What are the costs and benefits of going either way?

When driving your car, do you ever exceed the speed limit? Ever turn or change lanes without signaling? Have you talked too loud in the library? Have you let a co-worker use your computer ID and password?

We all have a sense of when to break rules, but in some roles the decisions are difficult and may take unusual courage. You may end up with a disaster if you don't break the rules.

In late October 2003, parts of Southern California were destroyed by raging fires. In San Diego County, the largest single fire in state history had burned nearly 300,000 acres, consumed over 2,000 homes, and killed 15 people. Other counties had similar losses for a total of three quarters of a million acres of destruction.

Throughout history, many tragedies have had pivotal decision points that, in hindsight, could have prevented the losses. This was no exception.

In San Diego County, a helicopter pilot was the first person to see the flames that would eventually spread and become known as the catastrophic Cedar Fire. He radioed for aerial water drops but the drops never came. State firefighters said the request came minutes after flight operations had been shut down for the night.

The helicopter pilot said he could see firefighting planes on an airstrip, so he made the call for help, but he received no response. At that time, 5:45 P.M., the blaze he saw was just about 50 yards wide and not spreading much. He again asked for air tankers.

But there was a problem. Under state guidelines, no flights can go up when it is dusk. On October 25th, the cutoff was precisely 5:36 P.M. with sunset at 6:05 P.M. Tragically, another helicopter with a 120 gallon dump bucket was within five miles, but was told to turn back. It would not have made a big difference by itself but the tankers never left the airstrip.

The guidelines were intended to protect the planes and, most importantly, the people who fly them. If you had been one of the firefighters, what would you have done? These events are instructive to a follower because it points out how hard decisions can be. Imagine an alternative scenario. The tankers are dispatched in violation of the guidelines. The fire is extinguished.

The news stories would have been quite different and all attention would have been focused on why the guidelines were violated. Few would have acknowledged the potentially huge fire that was prevented. Second guessing is pointless in such situations, but is routinely practiced by the media, politicians, and people who do not understand the situation, who don't like the outcome, or who get some value out of the publicity. That said, yes-you yes-now leaders know that such second guessing makes breaking a rule or guideline personally risky. It takes a strong person to choose what is right over what the rulebook says.

Do Your Job Well

"I'll do whatever it takes to win games, whether it's sitting on a bench waving a towel, handing a cup of water to a teammate, or hitting the game-winning shot."[28]

—Kobe Bryant, basketball player

To do your job well you have to know your role, what your teammates and leaders need from you, and what you need from them. This means you need to have mastery of the job skills and good teamwork. Most of all, you need the sensitivity to know when you're past your limits.

This last one is difficult because it amounts to knowing when to quit. Not giving up but accepting that there is someone else better than me to carry on. Most people have a hard time assessing their own performance while it is happening. It is much easier to be objective after that big meeting, after you asked the boss for a raise, after you talked with a co-worker about too much garlic at lunch, or after the big game. Even then, some of us are not capable of anything close to an objective assessment. This is a task better performed by others. This is often the boss, but better still, through a 360-degree process of feedback from peers, bosses, customers, and so on.

The 2003 American League Championship Series is permanently etched in history as one of the greatest baseball playoffs of all time. It matched the Boston Red Sox and their arch-rival, the New York Yankees. The stage for this rivalry was set over many years, way back to the curse people say was put on the Red Sox when they traded Babe Ruth to the Yankees in 1920. Competitive emotions between these two teams run high every year, a situation magnified by both teams being in the American League East Division. In 2003, they played each other 19 times in the regular season. New York won ten games, Boston nine.

So balanced were these two teams that the series was stretched to the final and deciding Game 7. They were now playing each other for a record 26th time. A Boston win would tie the season match-up at thirteen games apiece and send the Sox to their first World Series since 1986. On the other hand, the Yankees had won the World Series four of the past five years and wanted the chance to do it again.

Both teams brought out their ace pitchers for the game, Roger Clemens for the Yankees and Pedro Martinez for the Red Sox. This put two of the three best pitchers in Boston history on the mound, as Clemens had pitched for the Red Sox before being traded to the Yankees. Martinez had won three Cy Young Awards, given each year to the best league pitcher, and Clemens had won six. (The other best pitcher for Boston was none other than Cy Young himself.)

Earlier in the series during Game 3, both benches had cleared, players ready to brawl, after Martinez threw a pitch behind a New York batter, grazing his back. Martinez reportedly yelled something at the Yankees. The next inning, Clemens retaliated by throwing a pitch near the chin of a Boston batter, and the players of both teams ran onto the field. During the confrontation, 72-year-old Don Zimmer, a New York coach, charged at Martinez with arms flailing. Martinez knocked Zimmer to the ground.

Now in Game 7, Clemens and Martinez were matched up in a game for the ages. But Clemens tired out during the fifth inning with the score at 4-0, Boston in the lead. Martinez had been masterful holding the Yankees scoreless, but they managed to score a couple of runs in the next few innings. In the top of the eighth, the score was 5-2, Boston still leading.

In the bottom of the eighth, it all changed. It was clear that Martinez was tiring just five outs from sending Boston to the World Series. He had given up consecutive hits which scored one run, when Boston Manager Grady Little went to the mound. He asked Martinez if he could get the next batter out, if he had enough gas in the tank to get the job done. If not, Boston had a new fresh pitcher ready to step in. But Martinez said yes, he could do it.

Little left him in the game and returned to the Boston dugout, only to see that the real answer was no. New York got one hit, followed by yet another, tying the score at 5-5.

Grady Little made the call to the bullpen and sent fresh pitchers in. The inning ended with the game tied. The momentum had shifted in favor of New York.

What happened in that eighth inning? The leader (Little) deferred to the follower (Martinez) for a decision that was the full responsibility of the leader. The leader allowed the follower to make the entire decision. So the problem was all Grady Little's fault. Or was it?

First, a leader is better off if they get a practical amount of input before making decisions. Asking for input is okay. And in a veteran Cy-Young-caliber pitcher like Martinez, giving weight to that input is also okay.

So did Martinez really think he had enough gas to get the job done? Was he supporting his leader, and therefore his team, by giving an accurate assessment?

"He asked me if I had enough in my tank to get him out, and I said 'Yes.' I would *never* say no."[29]

Final score: New York 6, Boston 5. Yankees to the World Series, Red Sox go home. A yes-you yes-now leader knows the importance of doing the job well.

How You Spend Your Time

"I am requesting elucidation of my instructions ... 1) to train an army of uniformed British clerks in Spain for the benefit of the accountant ... in London, or, perchance 2) to see to it that the forces of Napoleon are driven out of Spain."[30]

—Arthur Wellesley, the first Duke of Wellington, seeking to clarify how he should spend his time in the face of requests for battlefield accounting of supplies

There are plenty of guidebooks about time management. Why? Primarily because our minds can generate ideas about what to do faster than we can actually do them. We also get plenty of additions to our list from co-workers, friends, and family members. So the to-do list gets longer and longer.

Highly organized people figure out the value of prioritizing their list with two major criteria – importance and urgency. Disorganized people struggle with this and often adopt either of two attitudes, "I'm overwhelmed" or "I don't care."

The issue is important for yes-you yes-now leaders because like the old saying goes, "You are what you repeatedly do." Choices make about how you spend your time define who you are, for both yourself and others. The fact that a person's time cannot be saved nor increased strikes home. Indeed, time is always decreasing and is unrecoverable.

This is not to suggest that a person should become selfish and please only themselves. To the contrary, a good follower makes choices that help achieve objectives, their own if it is a personal matter or their team's. Using criteria that answer the question, "Which of these alternatives will help us the most, short-term or long-term," will help you decide. Such criteria may include time, money, quality, or other key resources. In personal cases, qualitative factors such as friendship, helpfulness, or kindness may drive the decision.

When Carly Fiorina became CEO of Hewlett-Packard (HP), the issue of time management intensified beyond the demanding levels she had experienced up to that point in her career. She had developed effective time management techniques, both as a team leader and as a follower on her boss's executive leadership team. In public speeches and industry talks during her tenure at HP, she commented frequently about managing her time, saying "Since I became the CEO of HP, finding a balance between my life and my work is very hard, even with the support of my family. Life is a set of choices and you give up some things for other things."

With so many important issues to deal with, one of the hardest choices for her was deciding how to spend her time. She had faced a similar problem when she graduated from college with a degree in medieval history, uncertain about her future.

> So, I was planning to go to law school, not because it was a lifelong dream – because I thought it was expected of me. Because I realized that I could never be the artist my mother was, so I would try to be the lawyer my father

was. So, I went off to law school. For the first three months, I barely slept. I had a blinding headache every day. And I can tell you exactly which shower tile I was looking at in my parent's bathroom on a trip home when it hit me like a lightning bolt. This is my life. I can do what I want. I have control. I walked downstairs and said, "I quit."

I will give my parents credit in some ways. That was 1976. They could have said, "Oh well, you can get married." Instead, they said, "We're worried that you'll never amount to anything." It took me a while to prove them wrong. My first job was working for a brokerage firm. I had a title. It was not "VP." It was "receptionist." I answered phones, I typed, I filed. I did that for a year. And then, I went and lived in Italy, teaching English to Italian businessmen and their families. I discovered that I liked business. I liked the pragmatism of it; the pace of it. Even though it hadn't been my goal, I became a businessperson.[31]

Part of this is knowing that your criteria and choices will change depending on the situation. Fiorina's career change was both a product of the pain of how she was spending her time in law school and also the concern about how to spend the rest of her life. So criteria about how you spend your time require a tune-up every so often.

It's obvious that your choice of a meal when you were six years old is likely very different than when you are 30. Criteria change over time and we seldom acknowledge that.

"I think balance is different for different people," says Fiorina," and I think it's different for different people at different times in their life. There have been times in my life when my family got more of my time than work because it was important and necessary at the time. And this is a time when work is getting more time that it has in the past."

Take the time to create clear criteria and use them to decide how to spend your time. You will get better results for less effort simply by having clarity about the merits of your choices.

I Am a Linebacker

"You need to blame somebody! This is America."[32]

—Edwin Poole, law firm partner in the television show
Boston Legal

Fundamental rule: a yes-you yes-now leader takes care of their area of responsibility first. Then, and only then, should you look around to see if you can help someone else. The success of the team, your teammates, your leader, and your stakeholders depends first and foremost on you doing your job completely. No good comes from you helping someone else while your work falls apart. Everyone loses and the blame game starts. It takes focus and discipline to stay put.

❧

Imagine an American football game. On defense, a linebacker is supposed to protect a certain area of the field as defined by the defensive strategy. That is his first priority.

But if the linebacker were undisciplined, he would run all over the field trying to help. It wouldn't take long for the offense to figure this out and then start running plays to where the linebacker was supposed to be. The opponent's quarterback makes an easy pass to a receiver in the empty zone who then runs for a touchdown. The whole defense breaks down when one player ignores their basic duties. I once saw something similar in my workplace.

The loud voices in the office down the hall were enough to attract the attention of everyone on the floor. At first it was hard to tell if they were yelling at each other or yelling about something else. A few brave people wandered near the open door to see what the trouble was, or more likely to eavesdrop, seeking the juicy tidbits that make prime office gossip.

It didn't take much of a crowd for the two in the office to sense their presence, stop yelling, and close the door to finish their discussion. The only gossip conveyed was that Connie and Greg had a real knock-down drag-out, but no one knew what it was about.

Later that day I stopped by Greg's office to chat about a project he was leading. I really needed the status of the project, but knew the conversation would eventually get around to the shouting match with Connie. And it did.

Greg said Connie had come to him complaining about people on Greg's project team. They weren't helping her staff on her projects and not only were her projects not going well, they were more important than anything else Greg's team could possibly be working on. Of course Greg disagreed and started to calmly explain the importance of other projects and the criteria used for deciding work priorities. Connie didn't want to hear any of that. She just yelled more and wanted Greg to shift people to her projects.

After hearing Greg's story, I went to talk with Connie. It was the next day but she was still fuming. All it took to set her off was to ask her how things were going. She said she had so many projects out of control that she spent all of her time running to put out fire after fire. Many of the projects were missing deadlines and she was taking the heat for them. The latest in the series of misses involved key pieces of work from Greg's team. All she did was ask him for help and he gave her all this jabber about priorities for his team.

I went to talk with other project managers and found Connie had had similar high-tension conversations with them. It became clear what was happening. Like a nosy neighbor who minds everyone's business but their own, Connie was running around sticking her nose into everyone's projects to the neglect of her own.

As time went on, many projects missed deadlines. Connie was fired.

Are You Aware?

"I think self-awareness is probably the most important thing towards being a champion."[33]

—Billie Jean King, one of the world's great athletes and former tennis champion

Are you aware of your own actions and behaviors? Are you aware of other teammates' actions and behaviors? How about the leader's actions and behaviors?

The answers to these three questions vary from person to person. The answers might even vary for you, depending on the situation, and they may change over time. It is impossible to have an accurate awareness of everything all of the time, yet many of us try. That's fine until your lack of awareness leads to over confidence. Here are a few ideas that can help.

First and foremost, be self-aware. This is key because you can only directly control your own behavior. Your own self-awareness can tune you into being more helpful to your team. It also can keep you from undermining others. So start with yourself.

Secondly, be aware of your teammates and leader to the degree that it affects your ability to get your tasks completed successfully. Focus on your own tasks first. This is hard sometimes when another person's tasks seem more interesting and, well, you just want to nose into them a bit. But if you stick to your own tasks, you'll spend less time meddling in other people's work. You'll be much more effective.

Additionally, a yes-you yes-now leader will test their self-awareness with others occasionally. You don't want to become a pest by asking too many times, but a sanity check every now and then is helpful. Just ask people how they're doing and you'll be able to synchronize what they say with what you saw.

❧

Self-awareness comes more easily to some than to others, which may mean that you may need to work at it a bit. Sometimes even the gathering of facts leaves you with incomplete information, wrong information, or both. How many times have we had absolute belief that something was a certain way, only to discover later that what we believed to be true....was not?

There is a wonderful experiment about human awareness conducted by Dan Simon at the University of Illinois and Chris Chabris at Harvard. They showed people a one-minute video in which two teams of three people passed a couple basketballs to each other. One team was dressed in white shirts, the other in black shirts. They were allowed to wander about the small room tossing the ball to members of their team.

The people watching the video had one task: count the number of passes made by the team dressed in white. Not an easy task with so many people wandering around and two balls moving.

Suddenly, about halfway through the video, a gorilla enters the room, walks among the people passing the basketballs, thumps his chest, and walks out. Total time on screen: nine seconds.

Do you think you would have seen the gorilla? Most of us do, but incredibly, about half of the subjects in this experiment said they did not see the gorilla, even when asked if they noticed anything unusual!

The phenomenon has been labeled "inattentional blindness" and occurs in such common activities as talking on a cell phone while driving. We become so focused on what we are doing that we are not aware of other significant things going on.

In other cases, we become so convinced that we know what is going on that our lack of awareness guides our behavior. Recall the "He Ate My Cookies!" story that circulated through e-mail chain letters a few years ago. Probably fictional, but certainly a story to which we can all relate.

> At an airport one night,
> With several long hours before her flight,
> She hunted for a book in an airport shop,
> Bought a bag of cookies and found a place to drop.
>
> She was engrossed in her book but happened to see,
> That the man sitting beside her, as bold as could be,
> Grabbed a cookie or two from the bag in between,
> Which she tried to ignore to avoid a scene.
>
> So she munched the cookies and watched the clock,
> As the gutsy cookie thief diminished her stock.
> She was getting more irritated as the minutes ticked by,
> Thinking, "If I wasn't so nice, I would blacken his eye."

With each cookie she took, he took one too,
When only one was left, she wondered what he would do.
With a smile on his face, and a nervous laugh,
He took the last cookie and broke it in half.

He offered her half, as he ate the other,
She snatched it from him and thought....ooh, brother!
This guy had some nerve and he's also rude,
Why he didn't even show any gratitude!

She had never known when she been so galled,
And sighed with relief when her flight was called.
She gathered her belongings and headed to the gate,
Refusing to look back at the thieving ingrate.

She boarded the plane, and sank in her seat,
Then she sought her book, which was almost complete.
As she reached in her baggage, she gasped with surprise,
There was her bag of cookies, in front of her eyes.

If mine are here, she moaned in despair,
The others were his, and he tried to share.
Too late to apologize, she realized with grief,
That she was the rude one, the ingrate, the thief!

Being aware of your surroundings, what has happened, and
what is happening are key to being aware. Having awareness
keeps your judgments in perspective, reducing the chances of
your jumping to a conclusion that is not warranted and potentially embarrassing. Being self-aware and aware of your teammates
are essential parts of reaching your goals.

Children often do this better than adults and have yet to develop social inhibitions that stifle honest conversations. Curious about this, I gathered a bit of information – frank and refreshing – and compiled it in the Appendix. There you may see yourself through the wisdom of ten-year-olds and high school students.

Moments of Madness

"When times get tough, at some point, people instinctively know they need to lighten up in order to get through it."[34]

—*Allen Klein, businessman and music industry executive*

There are always plenty of things to do when you are part of a group working to achieve ambitious goals. What do you do first? And when it is done, what's next? The leader either provides the priorities or engages the group in a process to set them. This is fine for the high-level priorities, but as you define the specific work you need to get done, many more tasks seem to creep into play.

In addition to doing their tasks, a yes-you yes-now leader often has to cope with competing demands and conflicting priorities. One thing leads to another; what you thought was an easy task becomes complex; you keep getting interrupted; and then an emergency derails all of your plans. The pressure increases to get it all done for everyone, and the sooner the better.

At some point the walls feel like they are closing in. Your productivity drops. You get grouchy. You feel overwhelmed. You need a moment of madness to release your frustrations and lighten up a bit.

One day at work a colleague walked into my office and said he needed to talk about a computer problem. I stopped what I was doing, asked him to have a seat, and turned to listen to him.

He made a brief statement about the computer, but then launched into a very emotional rant, leaning over the front of my desk. The computers were always breaking, the system administrators didn't do their jobs correctly, the network was letting viruses in, and no one was doing anything about any of it. He couldn't get anything done because he was always fixing problems, so how could he be expected to meet the deadlines he'd been given?

I suggested we list out all the important issues he saw, so we wrote each one on the whiteboard. Then we went back to see what should be done about each problem. It didn't take more than a few minutes when he (and I) realized there was really only one issue of substance despite the list of fourteen things that we'd written down.

All the remaining issues were generated by the emotion he felt at that moment. We tried to understand what had happened and came to these conclusions:

- He had a long list of group tasks and individual tasks
- He felt pressure from teammates and me to get them all done
- He had internalized that pressure to create more pressure on himself
- When one thing went wrong, he saw nothing but doom and gloom

Our solution was simple. We recognized that we were both high achievers and put pressure on ourselves to try to do it all. Knowing that similar events would likely re-occur and rather than let the future issues explode, we started to talk about how to handle these situations better. Clearly the emotions needed an outlet, so we decided we would allow for a moment of madness.

I encouraged him to simply come in to my office and say "I need a moment of madness." Or I could say to him "Time out, you need a moment of madness."

Then for the next three minutes, he could say whatever he felt like saying, blaming anyone, saying rude things, whatever it took to release that pressure. Nothing in those three minutes would be taken seriously. When the three minutes were up, we would refocus and dig into the issues. And we agreed we would time the three minutes and stop exactly at the end of that time, not ranting for even a second more.

Not surprisingly, this worked wonders in two ways. First, he was now aware of his own reaction to pressure and could calm himself down. Second, when he really did get agitated and came to my office, we knew the first few minutes would be spent ranting. Not only did it get the emotion resolved, it became humorous. The unpleasant confrontation only months earlier was history, replaced by a quick, effective technique that left us both feeling good.

A few years later, I found this technique could work for different ages and in completely different situations. I tried it with my son when he was in grade school. One evening he was misbehaving at dinner. A series of reprimands did no good. In fact, they seemed to increase his level of combativeness.

He was getting so wound-up, I decided to give him a moment of madness. When we finished eating and had cleared the dishes, I asked him if he felt frustrated. He looked at me like that was a novel idea that had never occurred to him. He was simply acting how he felt, with no oversight of his own actions.

So, much to my wife's shock, I told him he had one minute to say whatever bad things he felt like saying, then we would talk.

I looked at my watch. He sat there with anticipation and joy, as if waiting for the start of a race. When I said "go," we could not believe the stream of swear words coming out the mouth of that 9-year-old. When I said, "30 seconds left," he started going so fast that we could no longer understand the words. It was a stream of gibberish, with a big grin on his face.

When time was up, he took a deep breath and looked very relaxed with a smile on his face. We got to the main source of his frustration very quickly and resolved it.

A moment of madness is quick and easy. It releases the tension, helps you see clearly again, and allows you to focus on the real issue.

Doing the Impossible

"Humans get trapped in modes of thinking and doing things. It's very difficult to be a Renaissance thinker like da Vinci, who could set aside old ways of thinking and look at things from first principles."[35]

—Peter Diamandis, founder of the X-Prize Foundation
which stimulates new accomplishments such as
SpaceShipOne

A yes-you yes-now leader must have a keen focus on possibilities in order to contribute to the goals of the team. Before something can be attempted, it must be imagined. All too often a follower will focus on their (or their team's) limitations, immediately generating a quick and lengthy list about why a task cannot be done. In doing so, they have short-changed themselves and their team, dooming their performance to a lower level.

The energizing attitude of the challenge from "I'll bet I can do that!" to the deflating disappointment of "I'm no good at that" or "We can't do that because ..." can make all the difference between success and failure. It is also a major contributor to a team having fun.

We have probably all worked or played on a team with people who have exhibited positive attitudes and seen how much can be accomplished. Even big hurdles are surmountable when people are optimistic. The opposite is true for negative attitudes, which destroy the ability to achieve and sap the energy of everyone on the team.

Young engineers, in common wisdom, are often given the difficult problems because they don't know they "can't" be solved. Experienced engineers have developed a method of assessing new situations to determine which solution path to follow. This method is effective much of the time, but limits creative, boundary-pushing approaches. Young engineers have yet to form such habits and are willing to jump in and give it a try. They often end up with a solution that works.

A good supervisor will also ask their employees to do work the employee may not think they can, to expand their limits by exceeding their own expectations. A yes-you yes-now leader can similarly have such expectations of their teammates. Even more powerful is when the follower expects their leader to take on new challenges, pushing the entire team performance to new levels.

When a task needs to be done and someone is asked to do it, the worst thing a teammate can do, either follower or leader, is to say "I'm no good at that" or "I don't have time for that." A fully contributing team player will work with others to figure out how to get the work done.

Mary Johnson was an extremely capable co-worker of mine but was predisposed to doubt her abilities and take the negative approach. Compounding the matter was her choice of associates. She isolated herself from other high performers and socialized with other negative under-performers. You can imagine what happened to Mary – her performance dropped and dropped in spite of teammates' encouragement to improve. She viewed every excuse for non-performance as legitimate and it became a self-fulfilling prophecy. Her entire focus became one of limitations instead of possibilities, with the expected decline in attitude, behavior, and performance.

Contrast that person with Carly Fiorina, former Chief Executive Officer of Hewlett Packard.

In the history of HP, nearly all of its top leaders have been very accomplished company men with engineering backgrounds. Fiorina was different, with a liberal arts education and a career in marketing. That gave her plenty of reasons to think that her limitations might keep her from career advancement at HP, to say nothing of attaining the post of CEO.

During her first day as CEO, she expected people would question her about her being an outsider and not being an engineer. She was fully prepared to deal with those issues, but was unprepared for the questions about gender.

> I made what clearly was, at the time, a very controversial statement: There is no glass ceiling. And people interpreted that to mean that I didn't understand that there were barriers and prejudice and bias. Of course I understood those things. I've seen barriers and prejudice and bias. But I said it because I believe that a woman or a minority can do anything they choose to do and can do it as well as anyone else.

I also said it because I think people who focus on possibilities achieve more over time than people who focus on limitations. Barriers and prejudice and bias are real; possibilities are real as well.[36]

What appears to be impossible may be simply your way of looking at your limitations rather than your capabilities. It may reflect your basic belief in your ability to surpass your self-perceived limitations.

Fiorina emphasized: "There will be people who see your potential and who take a chance, and those are the people who are smart – who know that the more talent they can use, the better off they will be and the better off the world will be."

She learned this as a yes-you yes-now leader throughout her career, eventually leading to her promotion to Chief Executive Officer of a multi-billion dollar company. Imagine what you can accomplish. Dare to do the impossible!

Steel Your Determination

"Luck is the residue of hard work."

—Author unknown

When working to take performance to a higher level, you, your team, and your leader will have the inevitable setbacks. Use them not for despair but to increase resolve to reach your goals.

This is something we expect from leaders and it is often said that if the leader shows any weakness or lack of resolve, the followers will pick up on it and the effort will fall apart. Now take a look at that from the point of view of the leader – to see the followers fall apart in the face of a setback with the leader losing their resolve as a result!

The leader is fully dependent upon the followers to fulfill their roles. If any one of them fails, the total performance of the team begins to get worse and the team may disintegrate.

It is a very personal challenge to be confronted with a seemingly overwhelming obstacle looming large, and you without the time or resources to take it on. One thing is certain: If you give up, you have no chance of succeeding. Therefore, the only logical option is to use your capabilities as a creative yes-you yes-now leader to tackle the problem. Even if your odds seem low, they are better than zero.

Your teammates and leaders depend on you to steel your determination, overcome the obstacle, and reach your goal.

ॐॐॐ

There are dramatic stories of people overcoming obstacles through their own determination. Many have been documented in books, magazine articles, television programs, or made into movies. They present the seemingly insurmountable obstacles and show the strength of people to overcome them, against all odds and logic.

Take a look at a team example, the United States hockey team's gold medal in the 1980 Olympics. The dramatic victory over the fabled Soviet Union team was immediately accessible to millions via television, promptly analyzed by many news programs, and eventually more thoughtfully explored in stories, books, a television documentary *Do You Believe In Miracles?*, and a major motion picture, *Miracle on Ice*. Theirs was a team achievement, made possible by the contributions of each follower as well as their coach.

An individual example was Aron Ralston, the fellow who was climbing in Canyonlands National Park and got his arm pinned between rocks. To survive, he made the decision to amputate his arm, and then hike out of the rocky terrain. How many people would have even considered cutting off their own arm? Of those few, how many would have dismissed it as sure death from either bleeding or shock?

Take the individual determination seen in either case, direct it towards a noble goal, whether it's winning a game or saving your life, and each follower has become a leader in his or her own right. The decision to take on the challenge with mental toughness is yours alone.

A few years ago, a young woman in Arkansas named Kelli Beaver showed strength of choice and determination beyond her 17 years. Her older sister had chosen the wrong friends, started using drugs, and eventually dropped out of high school and became a patient in a rehab clinic. When Kelli was 18, her parents divorced.

Kelli's response? She continued to play basketball, softball, and run cross-country. In addition to being a rare three sport athlete, her grades in school remained excellent.

She took the unusual step of transforming her role in the family from the child to a yes-you yes-now leader when no one else could find the strength. She became an example, both within her family and within her team.

But Kelli just shrugged off what to most would seem a remarkable achievement. "I took it, dealt with it and said, 'This is reality,' you can't just quit because you have to go through something hard."

Leading
Your Team

Create Perfect Harmony

"Life isn't about finding yourself, it's about creating yourself."[37]

—George Bernhard Shaw, critic and playwright, winner of
the 1925 Nobel Prize for Literature

The creation of perfect harmony is a noble goal which is seldom reached if your team is working on anything complex and demanding. You may sometimes debate decisions, even with yourself, and it is nearly certain that you will have moments of dissent and conflict with more than one person involved.

Perfect harmony is not the total avoidance of problems, but rather having ways to productively work out problems as they arise. As in many roles of the yes-you yes-now leader, this means keeping the goal in mind, not just your own reaction, when choosing your actions.

As the follower-leader relationship develops or as the roles of the leader and follower shift back and forth, the occasions for using productive problem solving will become fewer and fewer as people fall into comfortable roles. They begin to feel that problem solving is no longer necessary in the relationship.

This is a very fragile state if conflict does arise. One person may have unnecessary concern, thinking the relationship was past having problems. They think, "Here we go again." Another person may ignore the danger signs and blow right past a problem that needs attention. An effective partnership recognizes that anything can come up at any time. The commitment to each other and to the goal will pull the people through.

The ability of a group of people to develop the commitment to shift roles as necessary is an art form that must be learned. Beginner music groups don't have this, but the ability to create such harmony is seen in professional performers who have a well-developed intertwining rapport.

$$\approx \infty$$

Take a moment to recall either playing in your junior high school band or listening to your child's band. Remember the splats of the trombones, the goose-like honks from the clarinets, and the drumbeat that was just a half-count behind? In seventh grade beginning band we were all having problems dealing with our own instruments. We didn't have a tremendous sense of the whole band creating a unified song for a concert.

Then in eighth and ninth grades, we began to master our own basics and become aware of the players sitting around us – the woodwinds down there, the trumpets on the far side, the percussion in the back. As our awareness increased, we could hear when someone skipped a beat. It would throw the whole band off and the conductor would stop everyone, direct us back to a certain place in the music, and two-three-four-one ... we were off again.

Eventually, our sense of these minor events became nearly unconscious. One by one we crossed a nearly magical threshold. We automatically compensated for the mistakes of our teammates or our leader, creating a unified, harmonious performance that flowed like the rise and fall of the tide.

As we became more accomplished, the distinction between follower and leader became a moving target. Sometimes we were in one role, then the other, then someone else was the leader as the music followed its course.

The height of this follower-leader dance is seen in the classical music performances of the Eroica Trio, a team of a cellist, violinist, and pianist. The three women, Sara Sant'Ambrogio, Adela Pena, and Erika Nickrenz, have a lot going for them as they play to packed concert halls throughout the world. They have a smooth marketing campaign behind them and they are beautiful, attracting the comment that they all "look like supermodels" from a reviewer.

However it is their music that wins over the audiences and the reviewers because they so skillfully follow and lead as the musical score guides them along. Some of the published reviews describe the rapport achieved by these women:

> The Eroica musicians form one of the most exciting groups on the classical stage. It was a joy to watch cellist Sara Sant'Ambrogio begin the theme of the spirited Allegro movement, then pass it seamlessly to violinist Adela Pena and have it picked up by pianist Erika Nickrenze. The eye contact between Sant'Ambrogio and Pena seemed to contain every technical detail of the music they passed between them ... By necessity, pianist Nicrenze faces away from the other two, but they are so well-

connected through their ears, it hardly matters. – The Seattle Times[38]

Each musician is an internationally recognized soloist in her own right, and this made for an extraordinary group dynamic. No one was subservient and no one was dominating. They each gave a fullness of dramatic expression to the music.

It was a delight to see the rapport between these players. Their music breathed a deep understanding of each other and the many different relationships that exist in the music.

With refinement and technical brilliance and wonderful unanimity of spirit, this group exists in very rarefied company. These players have learned to breathe the same air, to carry on phrases from each other with perfect accord.

Even on a purely visual level, one notices a special harmony between them. The resulting music is balanced and sophisticated. – Frankfurter Allgemeine Zeitung[39]

Just as in their Carnegie Hall debut and smash hit CD release, these women demonstrate that on musical merits they have earned their foothold on the highest run of the profession. - Wall Street Journal[40]

Theirs is the highest form of the creation of perfect harmony, where each person is at times a follower and at times a leader, knowing which is which, and transitioning through these roles smoothly and seamlessly.

The progression from a junior high band to the Eroica Trio is something that is rarely done, but is nonetheless the goal for follower-leader relationships. Coming close to an Eroica Trio-like level of rapport and the commitment to shift roles should be the goal of every team.

Giving Your Consent to the Team

"Kareem took his great ability to score and sublimated it for the greater good of the team. He was willing to do that. But if either he or I had allowed that scoring ability to dominate, we would have cut down on the contributions of others to the detriment of the team. Kareem put the team ahead of himself."[41]

—John Wooden, legendary coach and teacher

"Giving your consent" to the team means you are willing to personally contribute to the objectives of the team, for the good of the team. Not in return for a job or for more money or for social pleasures, but for the good of the team. Following by consent gives power to yourself, the team, the leader, and the objectives you are all working to achieve. Simply put, you are voluntarily agreeing to do whatever is needed to be successful.

By adopting the approach of focusing on team achievement over individual achievement, you and your team are freed to focus on the larger objectives. Little or no energy needs to be spent convincing, persuading, coaxing, or forcing you to fulfill your role.

Consider what happens when you do *not* give your consent to the team. A leader or your teammates must spend energy on you, simply to get you to do what the team needs. This energy would be better spent on their own tasks to move towards the goals, not forcing you off dead center to do yours. The leader of the group needs to shift leadership style from leading-by-consent to leading-by-force.

If you, as the follower, are creating the conditions to require leading-by-force, ask yourself why. There may be significant people or performance issues for the team to deal with. You may be out of step with the group, diverting people from their tasks and goals without merit.

People will not follow leadership-by-force for very long, which means your progress towards team objectives will slow down and eventually stop. History is littered with the relatively short reign of leaders and followers who adopt an approach of force over consent.

><

Tom Brady is a fine example of a follower who gave his consent to his team. Brady plays quarterback for the New England Patriots of the National Football League. And he plays that position very well, contributing to three Super Bowl victories in four years from 2002 through 2005.

It would be easy to call Brady a star and the leader of the team, which he may be at certain moments. But that is not why he excels or why his team excels.

He was named Sports Illustrated's Sportsman of the Year for 2005. The article in the magazine was titled "The Ultimate Teammate." It said "his greatest achievement grows out of a generosity of spirit." Not from eluding defenders and throwing touchdown passes but from a generosity of spirit, crediting his team for their successes as Charles Pierce reported in the December 12, 2005 issue of the magazine.

He has defined himself, always, as part of a team, and that's carried over into this year, when his celebrity caught up with his achievement. He re-signed for considerably less money than the market might've borne so the Patriots would have maneuvering room under the salary cap. When Sports Illustrated's Peter King asked him about it last February, Brady said, "Is it going to make me feel any better to make an extra million? That million might be more important to the team." This isn't sports-talk-radio posturing. That's not the audience at which Brady aimed it. He was talking here to the other people in the New England locker room, none of whom will be making $60 million over the next six years as he will.

Brady is often compared to another NFL quarterback, Peyton Manning. The two shared the cover of Sports Illustrated on November 7, 2005. The article in that issue described the similarities they shared – competitive, never satisfied, and team oriented. Even though they play on different teams and occasionally those two teams meet in a game, Brady and Manning follow each other's careers, learning from each other. The Sports Illustrated article told of some of their similarities.

"He's similar to me in that he's never really satisfied," Brady has said. "I'm always interested in how he's doing and in a strange way I kind of root for him too." Each is a good, sincere man who is secure enough to feel a genuine appreciation for a fellow legend in the making. They've bonded over beers and congratulatory emails;

they've compared notes on handling the trappings of celebrity; they love each others' work.

The most telling observation comes from Tom Brady himself, describing why he plays football. "All I wanted was the camaraderie, to share some memories with so many other guys. I mean, if you choose to alienate yourself or put yourself apart, you know, play tennis. Play golf."

Most of us play or work on a team. Give the team your consent.

A Path to Good Group Decisions

"It's our choices that show what we truly are, far more than our abilities."[42]

—Albus Dumbledore, headmaster at Hogwarts School

A fork in the path will commit you to choosing one direction or another. Once you've chosen, it is difficult or impossible to get back to the fork without spending a lot of time and energy, so making a good decision in the first place is important.

So how does a group make good decisions? It could be the boss or the coach who calls the shots. Sometimes this works well but other times, the followers have the true expertise on the issue. A decision can only be reached by including those who have experience in different aspects of the decision. Mind you, these are not opposite opinions about the same thing, but instead are thoughts about the situation from a completely different viewpoint.

Imagine planning a trip. One person knows trains, another knows planes, and another knows automobiles.

All can get you to your destination, but each has a number of characteristics to be considered. Take travel time for one. The value of a fast or slow trip depends upon the criteria you have. If you want to see scenery, car or train is best. If you also want to read and take naps, the train looks even better.

A good follower endorses a process that will make these trade-offs clear and allow the group to come to an informed decision on their course of action. Many conflicts and unproductive decisions arise from people jumping to conclusions and making decisions based on only a fragment of the factors at play.

অ⚯ও

A few years ago I became the Chief Technology Officer at one of the most prestigious medical schools and hospital complexes in the world. Our mission was noble: to improve health by providing outstanding healthcare, advancing medical knowledge, and preparing tomorrow's physicians and scientists.

Yet when I arrived, I saw very smart, capable people working in conflict. Even simple decisions were made without thinking of anyone else, let alone what objective they were trying to achieve. There was little attempt to connect choices, made during everyday work, to the noble mission.

Someone would make a decision, implement it, then spend countless hours in meetings, hallways, and on email defending what they had done. Controversy and arguments were common. I found myself, as a new leader, spending nearly all my time mediating disputes. I did this for a few months.

With the passage of time and careful observation, I concluded that these people were really quite good at what they did. They were knowledgeable and competent, yet their expertise was not improving the quality of our technology delivery to support healthcare.

So I sent out this email and watched for reactions.

To: All Staff
Sent: Wednesday, March 06, 11:31 AM
Subject: Decisions, decisions

It's become clear that we can do a better job making and supporting team decisions. I see way too many emails, conversations, and meetings dealing with problems that could be avoided if a good decision were made in the first place.

I am asking each of you to **shift your time and effort from <u>post-decision conflict</u> to <u>pre-decision team-spirited consensus</u>.**

1. Stakeholders - include people who will be impacted by the decision
2. Objectives - clearly state what you want to do
3. Criteria - clearly state the dimensions for evaluating alternatives, e.g. time, cost, skill set, performance, platforms, etc.
4. Weighting - not all criteria are of equal weight, adjust appropriately
5. Alternatives - create at least 3
6. Evaluation - look at each alternative USING THE CRITERIA and OBJECTIVES
7. Selection - of the desired alternative USING THE CRITERIA and OBJECTIVES
8. Supporting - the selection as a team, stick together and make it work. It was the collective best.

If these steps are followed, when a weakness shows up we deal with it because WE chose the best alternative.

Too many times, we've skipped the above steps, or excluded stakeholders, so when something goes wrong, we point fingers.

There is no perfect solution to most of our issues. We have to make good decisions as teams and support our decisions.
This **shift** will take some time, but **start now.** It will make us better.
Thank you and feedback is always welcome, directly or through our anonymous feedback website.

Steve Tarr
Chief Technology Officer

A few people tried it and said it took too long. I appreciated their feedback because, while it does look like a lot of work, it gave me the chance to clarify that the 8-step process can be done in five minutes or five weeks. It all depends on the complexity of the issue, the number of stakeholders, the number of criteria, and so on.

But once people saw that it worked and that it reduced inter-personal conflict, the 8-step process swept the department and its use snowballed. As soon as conflict emerged during work sessions, people said "we better 8-step that" – it became a standard part of our culture and language.

I've used the 8-step process in consulting engagements and in other hospitals. In one case, a team had to meet sales objectives. Having been a great salesperson himself, the supervisor wanted to tell his salespeople what, how, and when to take specific actions to increase sales. He asked me how I thought that would work. A few questions of mine revealed that the salespeople were very experienced and would likely resent being told what, how and when. I suggested the use of the 8-step process, which would engage the salespeople as stakeholders and tap into their experience and creativity. It would let the followers contribute and design the alternatives. The solution would be of their own making so they would work hard to make it deliver results.

With some trepidation, the supervisor took the 8-step idea to his team. They didn't like the idea at first, confirming his fears. His salespeople wanted to sell, not follow some process. But as he continued to explain his confidence in their expertise to come up with ideas as a team, they warmed up to the process and finally agreed to try the 8-step. I talked with the supervisor a week later and he said they came up with many excellent ideas. The followers took over the process. Most importantly, they were enthusiastic and committed to delivering the sales results. Four months later, right on schedule, they delivered.

The selection of a patient care process in one hospital also used the 8-step, bringing an actionable solution to a problem that had been festering for nearly 12 months in spite of many meetings to resolve it. There were two keys to success: one, having the stakeholders create the solutions, and two, following all eight steps. Even seemingly simple issues can waste a lot of time if one of the steps is skipped. Much less time is spent following the steps.

Often forgotten, but most important, is step eight: support the decision the team made. The reduction of conflict and the peace and quiet on the team is a result of everyone having been through the process. If there had been a better solution, the team would have found it. With everyone included, there is no second-guessing and no disgruntled pot shots allowed.

Teamwork to Solve Really Big Problems

"Great discoveries and improvements invariably involve the cooperation of many minds."[43]

—Alexander Graham Bell, scientist and inventor

Much of what we do to be yes-you yes-now leaders focuses on our small groups, people with whom we are in regular, often daily, contact. We are only concerned with issues directly related to the goals of our group or to outside influences that may affect us reaching our goals.

Yet when it comes to really big problems, most of us, most of the time, throw up our hands and say we can't do anything about them. How many times have you heard phrases like "Let's not try to boil the ocean" or "Shall we define the issue a bit smaller than solving world hunger?"

When we look at the conflicts throughout the world – in the Middle East, in Northern Ireland, in the United States Congress, in your own hometown – which never seem to end year after year, generation after generation, it's easy to ask "Why bother?"

Some would say that conflict, born of conflicting goals, rational choices, and irrational behavior, is the lot of humans. They may be right. But what if they are not? Do we simply throw up our hands and let other forces direct the conflict to unknown or even random conclusions? People can accomplish amazing things if they have the ability to create the right team to solve problems no one could have solved on their own.

❧

Worldwide, most human disease problems happen in developing countries. The causes are many, such as swamplands that serve as insect breeding grounds, unsanitary drinking water, insufficient food and nutrition, and human infectious diseases with no methods of prevention. And the interrelationships between these different factors are complex.

In many cases, the causes themselves are too hard to fix, but the symptoms can be treated before they create health problems in people. One way is through the use of specially developed pharmaceuticals, targeted towards specific ailments and deliverable via distribution systems that can tolerate many days of trucking on bumpy roads, high temperatures, and high humidity.

Pharmaceuticals developed by drug companies are expensive, taking a long time for regulatory approvals and sufficient testing for efficacy and safety. A number of the drugs may actually prove to be effective against certain diseases, but are not manufactured in large quantities because the money to be made doesn't cover the research and development costs, let alone distribution to the points of use.

In the United States these are called orphan drugs, products that treat a disease affecting 200,000 or fewer people. Even though a treatment exists, these people continue to suffer because it is not economical to bring these drugs to market. The

U.S. Government passed the Orphan Drug Act of 1983 to provide marketing exclusivity and tax incentives for orphan drugs. This helped a number of Americans, bringing over 100 products to market, but didn't address the rest of the world. Big problem.

Then in July 2000, Dr. Virginia Hale founded the Institute for OneWorld Health with a mission to develop safe, effective, and affordable new medicines for those most in need. In her years of experience with pharmaceutical companies, Dr. Hale had seen what happened to potentially promising drugs that have little chance to make money – economic reality caused them to get shelved.

Dr. Hale's idea was to create a pharmaceutical company that could base its decisions on worldwide need instead of financial demands. OneWorld was formed as the first nonprofit drug company in the U.S. She also saw that research organizations, such as universities, sometimes developed potentially useful drug therapies but were too academically inclined to apply them to the real world. By forming partnerships with companies and researchers, she thought significant progress could be made towards treating disease.

One early opportunity to test her idea was the disease visceral leishmaniasis, which is one of the largest parasitic killers of people. The parasite enters the body via sandfly bites, much like a mosquito, then migrates to internal organs such as the spleen and liver. At that point, it is almost always fatal. The disease can be treated by drugs that are too expensive for widespread use. And because the insects are how the parasite spreads, drugs targeting either insect or parasite encounter resistance over time.

A significant attack on visceral leishmaniasis is limited by the expense of developing drugs for a human population that cannot afford to pay, leaving charities and academic institutions to work on the problem. If they make progress on the clinical front, fielding the solution is stymied by the hurdles of scaling up to large quantities and distributing the drugs.

This was the type of opportunity that OneWorld Health was seeking. With funding from the Gates Foundation and by partnering with healthcare centers in India, clinical trials showed that an orphan drug, paromomycin, was effective. It was also inexpensive to produce, giving hope to a solution more effective than any before.

OneWorld has continued to grow and have success with its business model, and people all over the world have benefited. While Dr. Hale led the formation of OneWorld, she was followed by many other people and organizations, all of whom have teamed to begin solving the big problems of global disease. True teamwork was involved, with her experiences revealing the problems and the followers working to solve them.

Helping Your Teammates Become Better

"Make individuals feel important and part of something larger than themselves."[44]

—Colin Powell, solider, statesman, and former U.S. Secretary of State

A yes-you yes-now leader will not only work hard at their own tasks, but will also support other teammates in their tasks to achieve the group's goals. Other chapters in this book show how each person's individual efforts all add up to a strong team. It's a heavy load to bear if you're trying to do it all by yourself. A single superstar performer rarely carries the day.

To get high performance and strong team cohesiveness, a follower will work to support and guide teammates to achieve their best. Sometimes they do it unknowingly – that's just who they are. Other times they encourage their team explicitly, so everyone knows they're doing it. These different ways are illustrated in the following examples.

These are not the only ways to help others become better teammates, but you can build on these examples to create ideas that work in your situation. The most important part is to believe that you, as a yes-you yes-now leader, can multiply your efforts through guiding yourself and your teammates.

The San Antonio Spurs had incredible success in the National Basketball Association (NBA), winning the championship in 1999, 2003, and 2005. It is true that people like winners and winners bring out even the fair-weather fans. But in San Antonio, the fans adored their Spurs in a way that goes far beyond their championships. Fans have always been proud to say that the players and the coaches are so nice you'd like to have them over for Sunday dinner, and they would come and fit right in with the family.

Imagining such a pleasant scene is difficult with the reputation so many professional basketball teams have. A prime example is the on-court fracas in the 2004-2005 season between the Indiana Pacers and the Detroit Pistons after a fan threw a beer and a player charged into the stands, starting a melee that ended up with five players and five fans being charged with assault and battery.

So what is the key to San Antonio's success? Building such a team is a complex art and of course there are many factors. If we look at the values of the players, and a few players in particular, we'll see a couple of the key elements.

In the 2005 playoffs, Spur Robert Horry ended up a hero by sinking key shots in Game 7, winning the game and the championship. But the first half of his play in Game 5 tells us more about the man.

In that half, he missed many shots, didn't hold his position on defense, was lackluster in his movements on the court, and didn't contribute much to the game. Where some players would have excuses or just remain silent, Horry's self-assessment was simple and revealing. "I wasn't a very good teammate." Then he fixed it by playing his heart out in the 4th quarter and the overtime period, leading the Spurs to victory. Many sports fans called it one of the most remarkable stretches of brilliance in NBA Championship Finals history.

San Antonio player Tim Duncan reveals another side of a winner, much different in character. Duncan feels responsible for himself and the entire team's quality of play. He is a quiet teammate who can get emotionally down about things outside of his control, but also knows how to channel those emotions into support for his teammates. His hallmark is steely determination that can be seen on his face. He is all business and some say his methodical execution of fundamentals is dull. While other Spurs and many other NBA players may play out of control and throw the ball away, Duncan is that solid force showing everyone how the game should be played. He pays attention to detail and executes plays with precision. Both Horry and Duncan, in their own ways, were intent upon helping their teammates become better.

De La Salle High School in California holds the longest winning streak in American football, by any team at any level. They focus on fundamentals and crisp execution, but they don't have many superstars. In fact their school is about education, not sports. Their mission statement speaks to an educational community, education, and student dignity.[45] While the football team has made the school famous, football is not the identity of the school.

Coaches can only do so much to motivate and create the environment for high achievement. At some point, the followers must take on the task themselves. De La Salle football players do just that. They lift weights year-round and it becomes the thing to do. "Everyone is doing it" is a powerful motivator for teenagers. When in the weight room, the encouragement is everywhere, "Lift, lift, come on you can do it. Yes!" There is only one coach in the room who does only one thing: blow the whistle to signal time to move to the next weight station. The followers take charge of getting the work done and explicitly encouraging their teammates.

Sometimes a yes-you yes-now leader helps a team and a teammate in a calculated way that no one really notices, but in a way that has major impact.

My daughter Emily once worked at the Coho Café, one of the nicest local restaurants in our town. As a new employee, she had spent time memorizing all the menu items, including the types of salad dressing.

One day a customer asked for a special Ranch dressing. The Coho changed dressings occasionally and Emily knew they had just dropped this special Ranch flavor. But instead of automatically disappointing the customer, she thought there might be some remaining dressing and she decided to go check.

Another more experienced waiter, who had a reputation for being cranky, had overheard Emily's conversation with the customer. Knowing Emily was new, he marched right over and quizzed, "Can you name all the dressings we have? Don't you know we don't have that one anymore?"

I have to say, with a little pride, that a lesser person might have been defensive and said something to make the situation worse. Not Emily. She simply went along with the waiter and thanked him for helping her out.

From that moment forward, the more experienced waiter was always kind and helpful. With one simple exercise of self-control, productive and calculated, Emily had established a relationship that helped her, helped her teammate, and helped her team to better serve their customers.

The common theme of these three examples? Self-awareness of the impact of your actions and behavior on the team. It is about the team, not about you. You just play a role, multiplying your efforts for the team, in a cause for the greater good.

An obvious way followers encourage their teammates is by cheering them on. It's common to see this on sports teams, but a work-related version of this is an exercise called Secret Buddy, where you draw names of your teammates and secretly note the positive things they do, giving them the feedback at the end of the day.

This really becomes most powerful when encouragement is contagious; when it becomes part of the culture to cheer on teammates. With the followers fully supporting and motivating their teammates, the team's performance improves. It also frees up the leaders to be more effective in their roles.

Demand Excellence

"The secret of joy in work is contained in one word - excellence. To know how to do something well is to enjoy it."[46]

—*Pearl Buck, author and Nobel Prize winner*

Each team needs to define its own expectations of team members. These shouldn't be what "we've always done around here." Nor should they be defined top-down from the formal leader. The key is to have a work session where the team members create a set of mutual expectations for everyone, regardless of their role.

This list of expectations should be few and simple because they need to be the core of the team's belief system. Eventually, living and acting by them will become automatic for the team, making simplicity a must.

అప్రా

Michael Kelly was my son's high school basketball coach. He was also my daughter's English teacher, following in the mold of famous UCLA coach John Wooden who also taught English and basketball. These men consider themselves teachers above anything else, regardless of the subject matter.

Coach Kelly emphasized the team concept. There was an excellent player moving into the area and part of his family's home purchase decision was the high school for their son. The dad and the ballplayer talked with a number of coaches. One coach said he would coach his team around this talented player, helping him build statistics that would get the attention of college coaches and that coveted big school scholarship.

Kelly talked with them and explained the team concept; that it wins games and also gives young people valuable life skills working with others to achieve success. And there is no designated star. A player that is good will have impressive stats within the framework of the team, not at the expense of the team. The young man chose to go the other high school and indeed became their star but that team didn't do very well.

When Coach Kelly started basketball practices in late fall, he gave his team the assignment to come up with their team goals. Then he left the room – a true commitment to letting the followers become the leaders. The players took their ideas, argued, listened, and hammered their individual views into a basic set of expectations for the team and for each of them. Here is what they created, and what they believed in.

Demand Excellence
Insisting all teammates execute their role to the best of their ability
Handle adversity
Self-starter

No Excuses
Accepting responsibility for our actions
Move past/let go
Pick each other up

Play Hard

Maximizing our enjoyment through complete effort
Mentally
Not 'surviving' practice

Michael Kelly moved from our high school to become head coach at the Seattle Preparatory High School. In his first season there he coached a team with Martell Webster, a senior who went directly to the NBA, and Spencer Hawes, a junior and a highly recruited player who signed to play college ball with the Washington Huskies and was later drafted into the NBA. Seattle Prep's team didn't make it to the state tournament that year.

In that first year, Coach Kelly was not able to implement his "team first" philosophy. I recall watching Seattle Prep in pre-game warm-ups with Webster warming up alone at one basket while his teammates warmed up at another. It seemed very unusual because the team ethic is not about one player, but about all people on the team.

The second year, the players understood the team concept and Kelly was able to implement better discipline. But a key was when the players themselves decided to be a team, as they showed by purposely choosing the same type of basketball shoe to wear in games. By doing this, they set their own standard and showed they had learned their lesson from the previous year. The result: Seattle Prep not only went on to play in the state tournament, but also won the state championship that year.

Coach Kelly had great players on his team the first year. Webster went on to be drafted by the Portland Trailblazers where he started 18 games – from small high-school gymnasiums to the huge arenas of the NBA in just one year.

But a great player and a great young man could not carry his high school team alone. It took the genius and perseverance of Coach Kelly to mold a team that worked together. And it took the yes-you yes-now leaders, the players themselves, who learned that success comes from having high expectations and demanding excellence of yourself and your teammates.

Stress Reveals

"You would develop test scenarios to properly load/stress the system in a test environment, and would monitor/debug performance and stability problems."

—Google ad for hiring a system tester

Systems reveal their true capabilities and inner workings when under stress. In the quote above, replace the word "system" with "truck" or "airplane" and the role of stress in anything's performance becomes clear. As a yes-you yes-now leader, you will observe your leader, teammates, and the entire group reacting to stress. Some keep their performance up and others fall apart.

In the course of working towards your goals, some tasks are completed more easily than others. People seem happy and are good teammates when all is going well. It is a common time to hear people saying, "I really like my job." Then a project stalls or a customer complains and the happiness is gone.

Think of a sports team. When the team is winning, the stands are full. But when they are losing, fair-weather fans stay home. Fans' true commitment to support the team is evident when they are always there, win or lose.

Similarly, many wedding vows have a phrase like "for better or worse, for richer or poorer, in sickness and health" which is spoken freely, then discarded when "worse," "poorer," or "sickness" really happens.

What these examples really mean is that people reveal their true selves when they are under stress. So do teams and organizations. So do machines. So does the environment. Each is a system that responds to stresses by either getting stronger or by breaking under the load, revealing its true capabilities.

A kitchen appliance, such as a blender, may do fine as you puree fruit. But put ice in it and the blades may jam. An old car may easily take you to the neighborhood store but will shake and shudder on the expressway.

Push any system – belief, social, biological, mechanical – to its limits and you will find its true capabilities.

⧼⧽

It is hard to explain why some people confront stress without falling apart, while others hide or run away from the stress as well as their responsibilities. But it is easy to see. Two contrasting stories show this.

Many years ago I watched a high school basketball game, touted to be a match-up of strong teams with very different capabilities. Both were possible contenders for a berth in the state tournament.

The Short team had a dynamic player only five feet seven inches who handled the basketball like it was part of him and could shoot three-pointers with amazing accuracy. The Tall team was anchored by a six foot ten inch player, who could dominate the area around the basket, scoring points, blocking shots, and grabbing rebounds.

The game went into the second half with the score very close. The intensity level kept rising. The Short team scored a run of eight points to open its largest lead. The pressure was on for the Tall team to close the gap when a strange thing happened. During the normal course of play, the dominant player on the Tall team fell down. And sat there. Then he slowly got up as the two teams sprinted to the other end of the court.

The player was not hurt but was not getting up to continue play. His coach called a time-out to get a substitute in the game. The tall guy came out and sat on the end of the bench, towel over his head, holding his ankle. No first aid was being applied. He didn't need any, for his ankle had not failed. It was his commitment that had failed.

He quit on his team under the stress of the turning momentum. He never went back into the game, leaving his teammates to battle the other team without him. They ended up losing by twenty points.

A professional football player showed a different response. When he was quarterback for the Green Bay Packers, Brett Favre played through the pain of injuries and the misery of addiction to painkillers. He has known much adversity on his way to building an outstanding career.

But the ultimate test came in 2003, when his father passed away one day before he was to take the field in a game against Oakland, critical to keeping the Packers' playoff hopes alive. Some people wondered if he would play, but Favre had no doubt.

He would play. But no one, not even him, knew just how well he would play.

The Oakland Raiders were prepared to take advantage of the situation, not with the intent of touching on the personal tragedy, but with the intent of winning the football game. When teams take the field, the game is every player's focus.

And so it was for Favre. He passed for an incredible 311 yards and four touchdowns – in the first half! At one point, he had completed seven consecutive passes.

It seemed that his ability to excel under stress came from his upbringing and personal choice. He did not dwell on his misfortune, for the team was more important. In a Sports Illustrated article, he said he never considered not playing after his father's death. He was raised to sacrifice for the team, whether it was football or his family. They were more important than any one individual. Favre told the sportswriter, "My dad wouldn't have stood for any excuses. In tough times, players play."

Calmness is Contagious

"Calmness is the cradle of power."[47]

—J.G. Holland, 19th century poet and novelist

Have you ever watched a flock of birds fly or the movements of a school of fish? The motion is very well coordinated and the group of animals appears to move as one unit. They pick up subtle cues from each other to synchronize their group.

Similarly, people pick up on behavioral cues from their leader and teammates. A good follower's actions play with the group's actions to achieve the current goal. But if you're the bird that turns right when the flock turns left, someone – like you – is going to get hurt.

While we often think the formal leader sets the tone, yes-you yes-now leaders can also set it for the group, or can reinforce it sufficiently to get the desired results. If the leader struggles or makes a mistake, teammates can compensate to keep the situation calm. No matter what, a yes-you yes-now leader can set an example for the team and the formal leader. In an interesting way, you assume very constructive power by doing this.

During times of high performance, calmness with the goal in mind is critical. Anxiety in small amounts is natural and productive, but too much becomes destructive by pushing you past calm purposeful execution into a panic-like frenzy. Your leader and teammates will respond to either cue, calmness or panic. Be an effective yes-you yes-now leader and choose calmness.

❧∽❧

A few years ago I witnessed a very powerful real-life demonstration of choosing calmness. In fact it was the formal leader who started the calmness, but each follower replicated the calmness with amazing results. As a result, it was a high performing team.

The 2001 Washington State High School Basketball Tournament had 16 teams in it as it does every year. But this year, one team was special. The Kennewick Lions were riding a 54-game winning streak that spanned three years. They were only two games away from tying the state record, three from breaking it.

They won their first two games to tie the record at 56. Going into Friday night's semi-final game, a win would give them the record streak all to themselves. They had won all 27 games that season and they were playing a serious underdog, the 19-8 Redmond Mustangs. People felt Kennewick would roll to victory and lock up the state title the next evening.

But at halftime of the semi-final, Redmond led 33-22. Kennewick had trailed at halftime in other games and had consistently battled back. That Friday night was no exception, and by the early fourth quarter Redmond's lead had evaporated. The Kennewick Lions took the lead with five minutes left in the game.

Then Jenny, one of Redmond's leading scorers and rebounders, fouled out. This was a serious blow to the Mustangs' hope of an upset. As she walked down the court, her disappointment was visible.

Seeing this, Coach Pat Bangasser summoned Jenny's replacement to check in, then walked onto the court and met Jenny well away from the bench. He shielded her from the rest of the team and calmly said, "We need you to pull yourself together. You're done for the night, but the team isn't finished yet. You need to set the example that we are a strong team and make us strong by being calm."

It was sheer genius. If Jenny had gone to the bench and buried her head in a towel, her disappointment would have spread throughout the team. Instead, within the 30 seconds allowed to replace her, she regained her composure, took her seat on the bench, and became a cheerleader for her teammates. It is probably no surprise that the Redmond Mustangs stopped that winning streak at 56, beating the Kennewick Lions 56-55 in one of the biggest upsets in state history. And Jenny showed the calmness and strength of yes-you yes-now leadership.

When the Group Won't Budge

"People are afraid to rock the boat in which they hope to drift safely through life's currents, when, actually, the boat is stuck on a sandbar. They would be better off to rock the boat and try to shake it loose."[48]

—Thomas Szasz, Professor Emeritus at the State University of New York

There are times when the future of an entire group is dependent upon one or two people making the first move. This can happen when the group is presented with circumstances that are surprising or unusual and no one really knows what to do, so it is critical for someone to break the ice by taking action. Another example is when people think something bad will happen if they chance taking bold, but maybe wrong, action. People's perception of the risk, balancing the possible results with the cost of taking action, is what drives their behavior.

There is the old saying, that the best thing to do is the right thing, the next best thing to do is the wrong thing, and the worst thing to do is nothing.

❧

Years ago I was riding a commuter bus from downtown Seattle to our neighborhood bus station. We had a substitute bus driver who didn't know the route very well. He took the wrong exit off the freeway, sending us south on another freeway in the wrong direction. The bus was full of regular riders – and no one said a word. It was a bit eerie as the bus flew along and passengers exchanged uneasy looks with one another. Finally a rider ran up the aisle to tell the driver.

With many apologies from the driver and many sighs of relief from the bus full of riders, we took the next exit and corrected course, losing only about ten minutes. Evidently, most people were too surprised or too afraid of being wrong to say anything. After all, the driver always knows where to go. That is what we have been conditioned to expect by years and years of bus riding.

September 11, 2001 something special happened among the passengers aboard United Flight 93. That flight took off from Newark Liberty International Airport headed to San Francisco. With a passenger capacity of 182 on the Boeing 757, only 37 were on board. Four of those were hijackers.

The flight was scheduled to depart at 8:00 A.M. but was delayed until 8:47 by heavy air traffic. This delay provided a valuable time window for what was to happen. Flight 93 had only been airborne about a half hour when its crew received a radio message to be alert for cockpit intrusions. Two planes had already hit both of the World Trade Center towers. The pilots asked for confirmation of the message. That was the last time they were heard from, for two minutes later the hijackers took over the plane.

During the next 45 minutes, ten passengers and two crew members made phone calls which gave them information about the three other terrorist flights that day. This information gave these passengers what those on the other planes had not received – definite knowledge that their plane was destined to crash into a strategic target.

The passengers on Flight 93 formulated a plan to attack the hijackers, who had all locked themselves into the cockpit. Todd Beamer's famous words, "Let's roll," started the counterattack. Smashing sounds from recordings indicated that a beverage cart may have been used as a battering ram in an attempt to break down the cockpit door. Worried that the passengers would break through, the hijackers decided to put the plane into the nose dive that ended in a Pennsylvania field. All of the passengers and crew aboard were nominated to receive the Congressional Gold Medal for valor.

More than a medal, by taking action to divert the plane crash into an empty field rather than the hijackers' intended target, those aboard Flight 93 saved hundreds of lives.

The Team is the Problem

"One man can be a crucial ingredient on a team, but one man cannot make a team."[49]

—*Kareem Abdul-Jabbar, coach, author, speaker, and former basketball player*

A team is a collection of people with different skills, each required for the group to fulfill its purpose. This interdependence creates synergy to achieve things that one person could not. But it also creates bounds and constraints that limit the performance of the team. If that sounds a bit like a paradox, it is only because of our shifting definitions of purpose and goals.

The tighter a team is coupled, the more difficult it is to move or change one part without affecting the other. In a reasonably complex situation, the interdependencies can be so entrenched that the team starts to be good at only one thing or become so set in its ways that it looks like a bureaucracy. It can feel like one too, inside and outside of the team. It becomes almost impossible for any change to be made without affecting everything else, so no one wants to improve anything.

As teams evolve, interdependencies arise to meet specific needs but can and do persist for a long time. The phrase "We've always done it that way around here" becomes a favorite.

Let's forget the complexities of people and teams for a moment and focus on a simpler system. A home entertainment system can be purchased in many different forms. Let's say we want to watch television, watch movies using the latest technology (streaming video), or some older standard technology (videotape), or listen to music (from FM radio, CDs, cassette tapes, MP3s, WAV files, or whatever new twist has come out).

Go to your favorite home electronics store and tell them what you want. You'll likely get an overwhelming number of choices. For simplicity we'll narrow them down to two – an all-in-one product or a component system with one separate box for each of your desired features.

If you go with the component system, you'll tend to pick the best of each item – the best DVD player, the best amplifier, the best picture screen, and so on. Problem is, you're told, that if these are not "matched" properly, you won't be happy because the different components won't be compatible, making poor sound quality.

Enter the all-in-one system, where all of the things you want have been pre-matched for compatibility by the manufacturer, put in one big unit, and sold so you just "take it home and plug it in." You do just that.

About a year later, after the warranties have expired, the amplifier starts acting up. Everything else is working fine but no sound comes out. What do you do? With all the electronics in one box you don't have much choice. You either send the whole box in for repair of just one component or you toss it and buy new. The benefits of having it all work together as a compatible system now seem lost in the current frustration of losing it all just because of one haywire unit.

Getting back to people dynamics, I once watched a basketball team that was very fast. Players on the team could run well so the coach developed their individual strengths into team strength. They were faster than every team in the state.

Then they took a road trip to California, playing some of the top teams in the San Francisco area. They beat the first two teams they played, using their speed as their primary advantage.

The third game was a different story. The scouting reports on their opponents said they were fast, too. Their speed was evident during pre-game warm-ups. When the game began, so did the footraces, players streaking from one end of the court to the other in a constant blur of action. The opponents' small lead grew larger and larger; first six points, then 10, and finally ended at 14.

The team was so good at running fast and had developed that style so well, they never practiced for an opponent just as fast. They could have, for they had some very tall players. A bit of adjustment to a slower style with the tall guys close to the basket probably would have worked, but they were so tightly coupled as a running team that they could not change.

Of course you want to have a strong team of interdependent players, but you also want to guard against the onset of complacency or bureaucracy caused by tight bonds and inflexible relationships. Yes-you yes-now leaders can use their unique positions to keep the team from becoming the problem.

The Lone Voice in the Wilderness

"People who don't take risks generally make about 2 big mistakes a year. People who do take risks generally make about 2 big mistakes a year."[50]

—Peter Drucker, professor, author, and consultant

There comes a time in everyone's role on a team when something seems to be terribly wrong but no one else notices. Or at least there is no clue that they are noticing.

These are times that test character. Many questions arise. Is there really nothing wrong? Does anyone else notice, but are they also reluctant to speak up? What are the risks of speaking up? Are there any benefits? What if I'm wrong? What if I alienate my teammates? What if I irritate my leader?

Being the lone voice in the wilderness is indeed lonely. There is no prescription for knowing when to speak up or how to act. Clearly one's internal threshold must be crossed to provide enough motivation to take the risk of stepping out of line.

As with all team-oriented actions, the goal must be kept in mind. Answer the question, "What am I trying to achieve by bringing up this topic and sharing my point of view?"

An easy way to get this started is by having the first goal to simply initiate dialogue, rather that trying to bring up and solve the problem all at once. This is important because, chances are you have spent a fair amount of time thinking about the topic, while few others have. They need time to think, too. Dialogue will help you assess the situation and guide the course you take.

$\approx\!\!\!\!\sim$

Sometimes I've wondered how on earth new movies are released with the themes and content I've seen in advertisements. Even worse is having had the bad luck to actually watch them on the big screen. Who decides?

Alan Horn has been one of the decision makers. Horn has had to figure out when and how to raise issues he felt important, among an unstructured group of people who all have a say in the decision.[51]

Horn has pushed filmmakers to reduce the amount of foul language and to eliminate violence against women. He has questioned why a character needs to smoke on camera, like John Travolta's character in the film *Swordfish*.

His struggle is our struggle. We all know sex and violence sells, but most of us feel that a line must be drawn somewhere. What makes it interesting and complex is deciding where to place that line.

Horn has faced opposition from other people, for the entertainment industry exists not only to entertain, but also to make money. On both counts, that means giving the audiences what they will pay to see and allowing the producers, actors, and theaters to rake in the money. Thus we get "gangsta" rappers, reality television more like circus sideshows, and even religious movies justifying gratuitous violence so sickening that even people who had chosen to go to a movie with an R rating walked out of the theater in disgust.

Some argue that if that's the way the story goes, that's the way it should be told. They all forget that the master of suspense, Alfred Hitchcock, was able to convey spine-tingling chills to the audience without in-your-face blood and gore.

So why does a guy like Alan Horn do what he does? His goal is to make sure that the activities and language are consistent with the theme of the film, while doing his job to protect the viability and assets of Warner Brothers Studios. He has to find alternatives, a common ground, to make both him and the filmmakers feel comfortable.

Smoking is a common debate. When the big-screen remake of the 1970s television show *Starsky and Hutch* was in script form, both main characters Starsky and Hutch smoked. Was that appropriate in 2004? Over the course of 30 years, the medical risks of smoking had taken root with a significant shift in American social values. Why would a new film have the main characters, the heroes of the story, smoking?

A compromise was reached. In a wonderful show of teamwork, the film's director, Todd Phillips, suggested that he'd have a couple of the bad guys smoke but not everyone in the movie. It struck a reasonable balance because a 2004 film with everyone smoking would probably distract from the entertainment.

Yet in the 2003 film *Matchstick Men*, the main character played by Nicholas Cage smoked cigarette after cigarette. Horn also challenged this with the director Ridley Scott but the chain-smoking survived. Scott felt it was a key visual expression of the neuroses of Cage's character's and made a good case for keeping it in.

Horn yielded on that substantive basis, but also on another basis which is key to being a yes-you yes-now leader in an unstructured situation. He said he just wasn't willing to ruin his relationship with Scott over the issue. Sometimes he won and sometimes he lost, but he developed a sense of when to push and when to back off.

Most importantly, he believed you owe it to yourself and your teammates to at least have the discussion. That leads everyone into doing the right thing.

Maintenance is Required

"Give up for a second and that's where you'll finish."
—Author unknown

The role of a yes-you yes-now leader is challenging, full of complex relationships with other teammates, leaders, and stakeholders. These relationships have their roots in a common purpose, which drives daily activities and interactions.

These are not sufficient to sustain harmony and constancy of purpose over the long haul. Team relationships are constantly being bombarded by events and dynamics. Some are within team control, but many are not.

Regular periodic maintenance checks are necessary to keep followers and leaders operating near peak performance. Without maintenance, relationships are bound to suffer, spiraling down and down until some conflict or crisis causes a major event to either damage or re-build the relationship.

❧

Most people spend more time and money maintaining their car than they do key relationships. They operate under the belief, often unconsciously, that the normal daily interactions with a person are sufficient to having a highly satisfying relationship. You'd never do that with your car.

Every car comes with an owner's manual and recommended scheduled maintenance, usually at 15,000 miles and so on. If you don't follow it exactly, your car will keep running but you may notice a drop in performance. If you ignore it forever, the car eventually falls apart.

I have known people who actually do just that – buy a new car and drive it until it quits working, then they buy another car. For them, it is easier to skip the maintenance; they are willing to tolerate the inconvenience of progressively worsening failures, tow trucks, and repair bills until the moment of total failure is rewarded with a costly trip to the car dealer.

Do you know of people who do that with people? Friendships come and go over small matters left unresolved. Assumptions are made about behaviors, with no attempt to verify or discuss, until those assumptions get locked in as reality.

Families fall apart, whether through something as dramatic as divorce or as gradual as dropping out of the annual family reunion.

Workers resign and move on to a new job rather than address issues in the current workplace. Nothing gets better. The worker never grows as a person or develops effective interpersonal skills. The problem just goes with them to the next place.

Now imagine what would happen if you had an owner's manual for a yes-you yes-now leader. It recommends regularly scheduled maintenance sessions with your leader, teammates, and other stakeholders. A real conversation, perhaps with advance preparation and structure, every few weeks. How is this working? What problems exist in our working relationship? How could we be more effective? What is coming up in the next month that we should prepare for, together?

A friend of mine lives in the western United States, as does most of her extended family. She has a cousin who lives on the east coast who never came to the every-five-year family reunion, held the last week of June when the school year ended. They assumed she wasn't interested in keeping in contact with the family, especially since she moved away right after her mother died of cancer at a very young age.

Turns out that the east coast school where she taught went through the end of June. No one ever knew this until one cousin asked her point-blank "Why don't you ever come?" What a simple question with a simple answer – she was still teaching school until July. All those years with what appeared to be a family relationship in a state of disrepair, when all that was needed was a little basic maintenance. The good news is that the family decided to change their reunions to the first week of July.

All of this goes back to a basic idea from science, the concept of entropy. The theory of entropy states that without the input of energy all order degenerates into disorder. Houses periodically need paint and a new roof or they will fall down like an old barn. Cars will fall apart, rust, and disintegrate like we see on old farms. Our bodies will get sick and hurt unless we eat to get energy and exercise to stay healthy.

And similarly, relationships will become unpleasant, unproductive, and eventually end just like we see on soap operas. Unless a yes-you yes-now leader asks the simple question that gets everyone back to the family reunion. Maintenance is required.

One Single Unit

"Let's be real clear what we're after here, alright? Team, team, team. Five players on the floor functioning as one single unit, OK? No one more important than the other."[52]

—Coach Norman Dale, from the classic film Hoosiers

Many years ago when life seemed simple compared to today, amazing things were accomplished by one or two people, such as the flying machines created by Orville and Wilbur Wright. As the world's societies evolved, more complexity and the desire to do more with that complexity means one person can no longer do it all. Now teams of people are needed to build modern jetliners.

Getting a group of people to function as one single unit doesn't come easy. Decisions about what to do, how to do it, and when to do it need to be coordinated with other people. That's why sports teams have workouts to practice plays, theater troupes have rehearsals to learn their lines and timing, and work groups have team building sessions. The benefits of coming together as a goal-focused unit are immense, but it can take a lot of maturity and perspective for strong-willed people to assume an effective follower role, putting the larger goals before their own egos.

The film *Hoosiers* has been called the best sports movie of all time because it is based on a true story about how an unlikely team worked together to become champions. But it is not really just a sports movie, even though it is about basketball. The basketball setting merely supplies the framework for watching a dysfunctional group of young men, a new leader, and their meddling families and town citizens, transform themselves into the unlikely Indiana State Champions of 1954. That is the simple essence of the movie and now you know how it ends. But there are more important lessons to be learned from what happens along the way than just the final score.

The movie starts with a set of dysfunctional characters: There is Norman Dale, the new coach with a checkered past; Jimmy, a star player who refuses to play; only five players at the start of the season; and a town culture of interfering with the team.

It starts to look an awful lot like a team you've been on, doesn't it? And I don't just mean an athletic team. It could have been a debate team, a band, a scientific team, or your office team; any team that started out with the need to coordinate individual efforts to reach goals that no single person could reach on their own.

In a particularly critical scene, the townspeople believe the new coach's methods aren't working and they want to fire him. "We don't do things that way around here" is their justification.

They call a town meeting to vote on the coach's dismissal, take the vote, and announce he's fired. Then the star player, having seen what the new coach has been building with the team the past few weeks, walks in and says he'll play. But only on the condition that the firing is overturned and the coach stays.

What did the star player, an 18-year-old high school student, see that none of the adults could see? He saw: "Five players on the floor functioning as one single unit, OK? No one more important than the other." He saw the power of individuals putting aside their own egos to work toward a common goal.

Norman Dale stressed the importance of the team in risky and sometimes costly ways. In the first practice, one senior mouthed off so Coach Dale kicked him out. Another player walked out in protest, leaving barely enough players to field a team. Playing a game with only six players, one young man decided to ignore the coach's game plan. He was benched, sulking by himself as the lone substitute. A teammate fouled out a few minutes later, leaving only four players on the court. The bench-rider got up to play and Coach Dale told him to sit down. He preferred to play with four players, functioning as one single unit, rather than having a fifth player who went off on his own.

The players, fans, and referees all thought Coach Dale was crazy but, in the end, the dramatic effect of playing with four athletes built the kind of team unity they needed for their ultimate success. Because of this and Jimmy's yes-you yes-now leadership, they went on to the post-season tournament and won the Indiana State Championship, the primary goal they had all wanted and earned – as one single unit.

Celebrate Your Successes

"When you participate in your team winning, it makes you very happy."[53]

—*Ichiro Suzuki, baseball star, after breaking out of a hitting slump*

When working to take your performance to a higher level, you will experience small successes. They will be few and far between at first. Recognize and celebrate them, noting what you did, building upon them for the next step up. They will become more frequent and will eventually lead to overall success if you take the time to learn and reinforce what worked well.

It is each and every yes-you yes-now leader's responsibility to notice and follow through on successes. You can't wait for someone else to do it. Often people expect the formal leader to be the one in charge of celebrations. And of course it is, but any member of the team can take the initiative to suggest a celebration. Celebrations can be a great equalizer and a way for the team to bond together. It can be easy because many acts of recognition are free, sometimes a kind word at the right time.

❦

Celebrations can range from a thank you note for a completed task to a trip to Hawaii for the entire sales team hitting their annual target. There should be a sense of scale relative between the accomplishment and the celebration. But the actual celebration may not matter as much as the personal touch of the celebration.

This connection is seen in basketball. A player gets statistical credit for an assist if she or he makes a pass to a player who makes a basket as a result of that pass. But beyond the formal credit, watch a game and notice how many times the scoring player points to the passer as they run back up the court – thanking her for the nice pass.

Projects have milestones to achieve and every project team knows they need to "fight for every milestone." Projects don't fail in one massive collapse. Rather, they get off track one missed milestone after another. Celebrating the achievement of a milestone is important to the eventual completion of a project because it reinforces the correct behaviors.

When projects are well structured, major milestones may be worthy of an expense-paid team lunch. But one major software project I led was so intense that time for lunch during the project was out of the question. We had food brought in so we could continue to work in non-stop shifts, 24 hours a day, seven days a week. So when the project was completed, we celebrated with both cash bonuses and a dinner party cruise on Lake Washington near Seattle.

People loved the money, but it was the cruise that provided the chance for people to be acknowledged and photographed by the ship's photographer. The time on board the ship was full of laughter, conversation, speeches, and awards.

Was it me as the project director who came up with this great idea? No, it was a superb project manager, Anne Smith. Anne had a keen eye for the people side of our work and knew we needed a way to relax after the intensity of the project. Thanks to her, our celebrations were timely and effective. I still have my picture from the cruise. Don't wait for the formal leader to plan the celebration. Show yes-you yes-now leadership by looking for progress and contributions from your teammates, and then celebrate.

Playing As A Team

"The healthiest competition occurs when average people win by putting in above-average effort."[54]

—Colin Powell, solider, statesman, and former U.S.
Secretary of State

A yes-you yes-now leader has a formal leader to follow, of course, but they also have a team to follow. We all know that great teamwork helps achieve great goals. Through teamwork, each person achieves more than they could have on their own.

Once one person decides to do their own thing, the rest of the team crumbles. The dynamics set in motion by one person can have disastrous impacts.

∂∽

One of the beauties of sports is that it all happens in full view, for everyone to see what works and what does not. I have coached basketball for many years and have occasionally seen teams with large leads collapse into defeat. More often, I've seen teams with superiority collapsing and losing not because of lack of skill, but because of lack of teamwork. Playing as a team helps you cause the collapse of your opponent instead of experiencing it yourself.

We had one year where the raw talent level of my team was a bit lower than previous years. We knew many of our games would be close and it would be the little things, the attention to details, which would make the difference between winning and losing.

We started the season with a five-point loss to an arch-rival school. It was bad enough to lose the game, but the other team had a penchant for screaming and yelling their (over) enthusiasm. Frankly, it was irritating. So to lose to them was maddening. Players and coaches decided that would not happen again. They would redouble their efforts in practice and games.

We won the next game, then another and another. None of the victory margins were large, but we had started playing together as a team much better. When the teamwork concept had really sunk in, we went out and played an entire game with that mindset. We won by 30 points.

Playoffs came and we had a tough road to the championship game. We worked our way to the semi-finals when, during the second half, our teamwork strangely unraveled.

We needed a new strategy. I knew they could not keep up with us if we kept the intensity up, so I called a time-out to set up a full court press. I told the players we would press the rest of the game, that we had plenty of capable players on the bench, and if anyone got tired or I sensed they were slowing down, I'd put a substitute in.

We went back out and pressed them all the way up the court. So far so good. The next time up the court, one player backed off and we pressured them part-way up the court; the time after that we backed off at about half court; then followed by only quarter court coverage. Each time, I called out to them to remember we were in full court defense. Nothing improved.

Somehow one player let up, and whether intentional or not, the effect on the team was disastrous. Our defense fell apart and our opponents were gaining momentum.

I immediately turned to our bench and picked five new players – you, you, you, you, and you – as I tapped their heads. As they stood up, I asked if they knew what defense we were playing. They smiled and almost shouted, "Press." The enthusiasm was definitely there!

At the next opportunity, five went into the game and five came out. As our five most experienced and capable players came off the court, I did something unusual. I stopped them as a group at courtside and explained that I had used a valuable timeout to set up the defense, and then they stopped playing it. I expressed that we needed team play to be successful and they had just done the opposite.

As I turned my attention to the game, my assistant later told me the exiting players had amazed looks on their faces. I don't think they had ever been pulled out of a game en masse like that.

But you should have seen the five new players! Yes-you yes-now leaders showing their benched teammates what to do, playing with enthusiasm. They excelled with pressure and teamwork. And after that group tired, I put the original five back in. They had gotten the message, loud and clear. They followed the instructions of their coach and the example of their tired teammates. We, the underdogs, won that game and earned our way into the championship.

We won that one too, playing as a team with yes-you yes-now leadership.

.

Leading
Your Leader

Loyalty Revisited

"When we are debating an issue, loyalty means giving me your honest opinion, whether you think I'll like it or not. Disagreement, at this stage, stimulates me. But once a decision has been made, the debate ends. From that point on, loyalty means executing the decision as if it were your own."[55]

—Colin Powell, solider, statesman, and former U.S. Secretary of State, speaking to his team upon assuming command of 75,000 troops in Europe

While loyalty works well when everyone is focused on the goal of the group, it is worth looking more closely at the relationship between a follower and a leader.

Is the leader articulating the goals of the group or the leader's own personal goals? Are they the same thing? How can you tell? Is the leader driving the followers to the leader's desired conclusion? Or is the leader guiding the team through an open debate that will lead to a conclusion serving the group?

When Colin Powell was Chair of the U.S. Joint Chiefs of Staff, he and his team had to deal with many issues for which there were no clear answers. There were numerous points of view, each suggesting very different courses of action. Given the impact of their decisions on the world, it was extremely important to hear all parties and make good decisions. He also recognized people's natural tendencies to work with a leader and also, sometimes, to stubbornly work against a leader. There was uncertainty about what the follower-leader agreement should be regarding loyalty.

The quote at the beginning of this chapter summed up his view on loyalty between followers and leaders:

> When we are debating an issue, loyalty means giving me your honest opinion, whether you think I'll like it or not. Disagreement, at this state, stimulates me.

During the debate process, followers assume constantly changing leadership roles as they take the floor to speak their ideas and positions. A follower transitioning into the yes-you yes-now leader role must communicate clearly and then know when to pass the baton to another member of the group. During this period of ideas and discussion, both followers and leaders have to work to keep the debate on track and to make progress toward the goal.

If at any time the formal leader starts to squelch ideas and debate, the desired goal will likely not be met. People will clam up and cease to share. Some leaders do this inadvertently by over-asserting their formal leadership role, even to the point of being demanding, aggressive, and yelling. Others do it intentionally, misusing the power of their role to get what they want, group be damned. Powell's quote continued:

> But once a decision is made [based on the group's open discussion], the debate ends. From that point on, loyalty means executing the decision as if it were your own.

Followers and leaders alike adhere to this on a strong team. If the debate is open and healthy, each team member knows that the decision is the best the group could create. Therefore they will implement the decision as if it were their own.

In this way, the balance between leaders and followers is maintained and the supreme concept of loyalty to the group's goals and ideals will take hold.

To say what you want during the debate puts the responsibility on the followers to be confident enough to speak their minds. The leader is responsible to create an environment in which followers feel safe speaking up.

I once participated in a workshop on inspirational leadership during which the facilitators taught the importance of speaking up. They asked if any of us had been in work meetings where we felt the urge to say something that seemed important but perhaps not in line with popular thought. The question was answered with a lot of laughter, each of us remembering all too well when this had happened.

"Have the strength to speak up," we were encouraged.

Towards the end of the second day of the workshop, we were asked to do a secret ballot vote. We were to write on a piece of paper Yes or No to the question "Would you be willing to spend six or seven days in a residential offsite meeting to further our group's growth in the area of inspirational leadership?"

A binary vote at that point was a problem for me. We had been through a day and a half of the material, which seemed fine.

But there were many unanswered questions. How much would it cost? Could we all afford that much time away? What about our family obligations? Did we have the right group of people? How much better would we be after an intense week off-site? How would we measure and assess value?

Given these questions, how could a responsible leader have a clear answer at this point? Yet that is what we were being asked to do.

So the facilitators passed out one small piece of paper to each of the 50 participants. When they came to me, I asked for three pieces. I started writing down the many questions, saving one piece for my actual vote.

I was still writing when the facilitator brought the ballot box to me. The CEO noticed me writing and said jokingly (or was it?), "C'mon, this is a Yes or No question, if you want to write that much, send me an email." (Hmmm, interesting, considering that previous direct emails to this CEO had gone unanswered!)

The facilitator holding the box also repeated, "Yes or No, just drop it in the box." She was beginning to look irritated.

Feeling the pressure and refusing to yield, I wrote Maybe on my ballot. I did not fold it and it landed in the box visible to the facilitator.

"Maybe?" she challenged, with a piercing look. "Has to be Yes or No."

"I understand, but there are so many unanswered questions for a commitment of this magnitude. I cannot responsibly say one way or the other."

"Well then, I guess your vote is a No," she snipped.

"Or it could be a Yes. I just don't know at this point. You are free to put my vote where you think best."

With that she moved off. I think I detected steam coming from her ears.

A few minutes later, the votes were tallied, written on a large easel chart. A lot of Yes votes, some No votes, and one Maybe.

The entire group was laughing, demanding to know who voted Maybe. I proudly raised my hand and repeated that there were too many unanswered questions at this point.

And I was only doing what we had been taught during the workshop – have the strength to speak up when something isn't right.

The laughter continued, all in good spirit. But in the last few minutes of the workshop, more than one person said that, had they thought more carefully about the issues and been a bit more bold, they too would have voted Maybe!

Leaders Don't Solve Problems

"Leaders create an environment which everyone has the opportunity to do work which matches their potential capability."[56]

—*Elliot Jacques, organizational development psychologist*

Leaders don't solve most of the problems in a team, nor do they discover what really works. The followers do. The leader's job is to create the environment for the team to be successful. Then the leader and all other team members operate within that framework.

When followers contribute to and work within that framework, the team is more likely to be successful in reaching its goals.

❧

John Wooden created an effective environment through attention to detail, from his early years as an English teacher to his years of coaching UCLA men's basketball to win 10 national championships. Coach Wooden was a master of planning. Every activity had a purpose.

It's no surprise that some people don't like such rigor. They are entitled to their preferences, and they are also entitled to the lower achievements that come with those preferences. Wooden made sure he built a high-achievement environment, but he did no dribbling or shooting. The players did. A big lesson for leaders to learn: you do not dribble and shoot, even though you know how to do both. Let your people do their jobs.

Coach Wooden prepared people to do their jobs by creating a productive environment, both for himself and for his players. For himself, he prepared meticulous practice plans so each skill was built from the bottom up, and each drill built upon previous drills. The players did not need to know this, and most of them didn't. They just did what the practice plan said.

Coach Wooden provided this example in his book *Practical Modern Basketball*. Take a moment to notice the precision, right down to five minute increments in some cases.

3:00-3:30	5 made free throws at 5 baskets; individual drills – rebounding, special shots, post moves, defensive positions, passing and cutting, shooting range
3:30-3:40	Easy running of floor, change of pace and direction, defensive slides, one on one, pass receiving, jumping
3:40-3:45	Five man – rebounding and passing
3:45-3:50	Five man – dribble and pivot
3:50-4:00	Five man – alternate post pass and cut options
4:00-4:15	Three man lane with one and two men alternating on defense

4:15-4:25	Shooting – forwards, guards, centers separately; footwork to get free
4:25-4:35	Strong-side defense
4:35-4:40	Ball handling
4:40-4:50	Offensive patterns – strong side options
4:50-4:55	Three on two conditioner
4:55-5:10	Team fast break; one on one defense
5:10-5:25	Half court scrimmage – starters on defense, then fast break
5:25-5:40	Half court scrimmage – starters on offense
5:40-5:45	Free throws all six baskets

Practice plans varied with the time of the season, the day of the week, and the number of days before the next game. The followers had to work within the master plan. There are famous stories about the first practice of the year, each and every year at UCLA. Coach Wooden had all the players in the locker room and told them to sit down. He then went through the proper technique to put on socks and lace up their shoes.

I picked that up when I was teaching in high school. We had a lot of blisters, and I found out that a lot of the players didn't smooth out all the wrinkles around their heels and around their little toes, places where the blisters are apt to occur. Then I found out that they didn't lace their shoes properly and oftentimes they wore shoes that were a size too large. With all the quick-stop turning, changes of direction, changes of pace on a hard floor you have in basketball, this would cause blisters. So, I thought it was very important that I'd check their shoe size and how they put their socks on. I hoped they would take a few extra seconds to smooth out the wrinkles around the heel and the toes and hold the sock up while they put their shoe on. I think it was important. And I know from the time I started in high school that we greatly reduced the number of blisters that we'd have, so I continued that throughout my coaching. I know a number of players laughed about it. They probably still laugh about it now. But I stuck to it. I think to some degree it helped team unity. I believed in that and I insisted on it.[57]

You can imagine how Wooden's attention to detail influenced the players' approach to drills, practicing correctly, and playing the game. Their execution was superb because Wooden had created an environment that allowed them to play their best possible game.

Coach Wooden made a significant contribution with his Pyramid of Success. It is probably the most widely distributed and used framework in all management, well beyond basketball. He developed it over a period of 40 years and still sends out over 1,500 copies a year – personally. Thousands more are reproduced and sold by others.

The main lesson here is for followers. It is your job to do your job, and you have a right to expect a productive environment from your leaders. You may become a yes-you yes-now leader yourself, within your team, in order to make sure this happens. Expect your formal leader to create the environment. Expect for you and other followers to contribute and support that environment. Expect yourself to figure out how to be successful within that environment.

Pyramid
of
Success

"Success is peace of mind which is a direct result of self-satisfaction in knowing you made the effort to become the best of which you are capable."

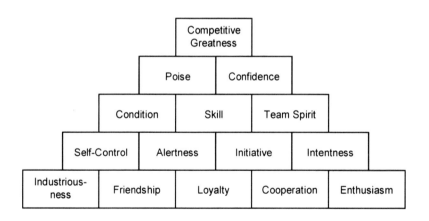

Pyramid of Success is used with permission from John Wooden and can be seen in its entirety in his books and at www.CoachJohnWooden.com

Great Leaders Begin as Great Followers

"At first the Army was something of a shock ... they were amazed that a Rockefeller was willing to do manual labor."[58]

—David Rockefeller, statesman and leader, recalling his decision to enlist in the Army in 1942

A person who can effectively follow a leader can quickly grasp the qualities necessary for leadership, enabling them to be a good yes-you yes-now leader. One important quality is to be aware of and responsive to the needs of followers. In fact, odds are that a good leader was a good follower, already demonstrating yes-you yes-now leadership. Why? Good leaders are very much in touch with the needs of their followers, because they were once followers themselves. As an effective follower, they were clearly able to see what worked and what didn't work, how to support their leader, and when to challenge their leader – all in the spirit of pursuing the group's goals.

You may have heard the saying, "He's a great players' coach" or "Our boss is great, just like one of us." These compliments are given to one who can relate to their teammates and lead them appropriately – not by being a dictator – but by understanding the role of the follower from having been one.

This does not mean a good follower *must* become a leader. Quite the contrary, good followers are key to any effective team and often are very effective in that role. They demonstrate yes-you yes-now leadership.

❧

David Rockefeller was born on June 12, 1915 into a family of privilege. His grandfather, John Rockefeller, Sr., was the founder of the Standard Oil Company in the late 1800s, a time when the Industrial Revolution and home lighting by kerosene were driving the increasing demand for petroleum products. The success of Standard Oil and the ensuing fortune for the Rockefeller family created the means by which future generations could live in grandeur.

While they lived well over the years, John Senior also began a family tradition of philanthropy. Among many accomplishments, he founded the University of Chicago, the Rockefeller Institute for Medical Research, and the Rockefeller Foundation whose mission is to promote the well being of mankind throughout the world.

John Rockefeller, Jr., David's father, inherited much of this fortune and the oversight of the various philanthropic founda-tions. John Junior's family eventually grew to six children. Their homes included one in New York City, a beautiful estate north of the city, and a summer retreat on the coast of Maine. David was raised in these places and had all the benefits great wealth could provide. Because of his grandfather's and father's values to better the world, David also developed an everyman sense of fair living.

These values came forth when in 1942, after earning a Ph.D. in economics, David enlisted in the army as a private, choosing not to use his family's influence to get a safe military job. He entered basic training, like everyone else, at Governor's Island, New York, on May 1. In his book *Memoirs*, he recalls:

> Basic training consisted of endless hours of close-order drill, calisthenics, learning how to care for and fieldstrip our weapons, and, of course, the inevitable KP duty. At first the Army was something of a shock. It was at once threatening because it was all so new and, at the same time, boring and arduous. I had entered the Army with serious misgivings about my ability to cope with its rigors physically or to adapt socially. I had never been a good athlete, and I was not good at most competitive sports. Thus, having occasional bits of time to play baseball was more nerve-racking to me than close-order drill. At the outset I wondered how I would fare mixing with people from very different backgrounds, tastes, and skills.
>
> As it turned out, basic training went surprisingly well. Submitting to military discipline and getting on with my fellow trainees was much less of a problem than I had anticipated. I had a strong sense of duty, of doing what I was told, and following orders was the primary attribute demanded of an enlisted man.
>
> I recall at one point that a few of us were assigned to paint the kitchen in the officers' mess hall. I followed instructions faithfully, painting quite a bit more steadily than some of the others who had a more lackadaisical attitude towards Army orders and work. It certainly wasn't my intention, but this impressed the officer in charge of the detail and also the other enlisted men. They were amazed that a Rockefeller was willing to do manual labor. I soon realized that I wasn't as inept as I had feared; that

I could get along and even become friends with people with whom I had few things in common.[59]

David Rockefeller later cited these experiences, as well as his wartime assignments in Europe and Africa, as being an invaluable training ground for much of what he did the rest of his life. As a follower in the Army, he experienced first-hand the impact of decisions made by his leadership, instilling in him a sense of responsibility.

Although he did not know it at the time and was apprehensive, his decision to join the army as a regular enlisted man, following the orders of his superiors, laid the foundation for his future success in leadership roles at Chase Bank, Chase Manhattan, the Council of the Americas, the National Council for US-China Trade, and the US-USSR Trade and Economic Council.

Not all who practice yes-you yes-now leadership become formal leaders, though it is not surprising that David Rockefeller, with his family history, became one. It is remarkable that he learned the role of an effective follower and applied it to his leadership. It shows the power of yes-you yes-now leadership.

By Your Pupils You'll Be Taught

"It would take twelve weeks for them to transform me from a college student to officer."[60]

—Gene Kranz, NASA Flight Director, describing the role his followers, new Air Force recruits, played in his leadership development

Yes-you yes-now leaders play an essential role in developing and sustaining an effective formal leader. After all, whom would the leader lead in the absence of followers?

But so often the dynamics of the leader-follower relationship is thought of, and practiced, as a one-way street, from the leader to the follower. In this model, the leader develops the follower. This is often called mentorship but could also be a standard hierarchical boss-subordinate relationship.

Yes-you yes-now leaders will take it upon themselves to provide a complementary flow of ideas right back to the leader. Direct guidance is one way; either the follower suggesting "this might work" or suggesting a specific idea that is better than the current plan. A more subtle way is when the actions of other people elicit reactions from the followers.

An effective leader spends the time and energy to observe the impact of decisions and guidance on the followers. The leader modifies the course of action depending on the success, or lack of success, of previous actions. In this way, the follower is demonstrating yes-you yes-now leadership by teaching the formal leader through honest feedback. This works really well when both roles are aware of the two-way learning that is happening.

❧

Anna Edwards was born in 1831 and had a long colorful life spanning 84 years. She kept a diary of her travels to India, the United Kingdom, Thailand, and Canada. In her later years, she used this diary as the basis for stories and books. Her most famous story told about the time she was a teacher of English in the Court of the King of Siam. Rodgers and Hammerstein turned this into a musical, *The King and I*.

One of the musical's songs is "Getting to Know You" which includes Anna speaking this prelude:

> It's a very ancient saying,
> But a true and honest thought,
> That if you become a teacher,
> By your pupils you'll be taught.[61]

Those last two lines have become widely used as a basis for education philosophy, acknowledging the role that followers have in developing the teacher as well. This wisdom is left up to the teacher in a traditional classroom, for what young student would have the insight to realize *they* are teaching the teacher?

But in the adult world, yes-you yes-now leaders can recognize and accept the role of teacher. It sounds odd, but it does work that way.

Gene Kranz was a mission controller for NASA's moon flights. Before getting to that lofty stage, he wanted to be a pilot and part of his career development included military leadership jobs. He wasn't always fully prepared for them, as he relates in his inspiring book, *Failure Is Not An Option*. In this passage, Kranz is a recent college graduate working various assignments while awaiting a spot in a flight training class.

By the end of my third month on the job, I was sitting with the test pilots and flight test engineers during debriefings, reviewing flight cards (a pilot's checklist for the test sequences), transcribing pilot's notes, and validating flight test objectives. Heady stuff for a recent college graduate and the next best thing to being in the cockpit. This experience would serve me well later when I sat with the backroom guys and reviewed our data on our space missions. At a glance I learned to identify the essentials and put the story together.

The months passed rapidly, and then it was time to pack up and report to Lackland Air Force Base in San Antonio, Texas, for preflight training. As of March 1955, I was now on active duty and assigned to pilot class 56M.

Other than St. Louis, I had never been west of the Mississippi River, and I soaked in the scenery as I drove through western Missouri and down into Oklahoma... I was a willing believer in Texas charm and hospitality as I drove through the gates of Lackland Air Force Base. There I would have twelve weeks of preflight training, a good part of which taught you confidence by putting you through some pretty physically demanding exercises out in the boonies. I also learned the essence of leadership through being given responsibility for raw recruits who were wearing a uniform for the first time and were badly in need of understanding why the military demands order in everything from the state of your locker to the crispness of a salute, instant compliance with commands, and other basic military cultural imperatives. As the song puts it, "by your pupils you'll be taught." It would take twelve weeks for them to transform me from a college student to officer, one hell of a speedy transition. It was the NCO's (non-commissioned officers) who taught me the basics – and my respect for the sergeants on the line grew with every passing year.[62]

Without the appreciation for basic disciplines he learned from those non-commissioned officers, Gene Kranz would not have developed into the effective leader he was. As a leader, he was mission controller for one of the most dramatic episodes of human history, the explosion aboard Apollo 13 during the early stage of its lunar mission. As seen in the award winning movie *Apollo 13*, many yes-you yes-now leaders helped Kranz gain the ability to bring those astronauts home safely. If you watch the movie a few times, you'll see yes-you yes-now leadership throughout the entire space mission.

Tough Talks Don't Mean Talking Tough

"Our senior officers knew the war was going badly ... yet they bowed to groupthink pressure and kept up pretenses ... the military failed to talk straight to its political superiors or to itself."[63]

—Colin Powell, solider, statesman, and former U.S. Secretary of State, commenting on the Vietnam War

Because they are tuned in, yes-you yes-now leaders often find themselves involved in conflict, ranging from the small and trivial to the large and important. It can be particularly challenging because they don't have the formal position power to deliver directives by talking tough and mandating one direction over another.

Lacking the power to "make it so," a person can take a number of alternative paths, two of which are avoiding the issue or addressing the issue poorly. Of course there is a third path of tackling the issue directly and reaching an effective conclusion. Guess which choice most people make?

We avoid difficult issues because we lack the skills to deal with them. When we develop these skills, our world changes dramatically. With healthier dialogue, we get better results.

There are entire books devoted to this topic. One of the best is *Crucial Conversations*.[64] A crucial conversation is needed when:

1. When opinions vary
2. When the stakes are high
3. When emotions run strong

Notice that these three items get progressively more difficult. Varying opinions is not uncommon and we all have some capacity to accommodate them. It gets a little more difficult when the stakes are high. Choosing where to go to dinner has lower stakes than choosing which car to buy. Add strong emotions to the mix and the situation can become explosive.

The two most important things to do in these situations are to listen and to make it safe to discuss the topic. More bad happens when people hold back their thoughts than when they deal with whatever thoughts they have. You can't deal with what you don't know about. Therefore, no tough talk. It will only make people retreat and withhold.

☙❧

I remember one particular piece of advice from *Crucial Conversations* because it is both humorous and powerful. Similar to "Don't drink and drive," it says not to engage in crucial conversations unless your adrenaline level is below the legal limit. It's hard to think straight when you are under the influence. So the first step is timing, knowing when and when not to start a crucial conversation.

Of course many things in life involve crucial conversations. Some of them are with yourself, such as establishing your own major goal or personal mission statement. These can be the most challenging because you likely hold many opinions about your abilities and you care a lot about the outcome so the stakes are high. And, if you're like most people, you're probably more rational about others and more emotional about yourself.

When a crucial conversation presents itself, there are three courses of action.

1. Ignore it and hope it will go away
2. Handle it poorly
3. Handle it well

Option 3 looks like a good choice but it seems that options 1 and 2 are taken more often. You know that crucial issues rarely go away and you will just have to deal with it later, at which time the situation may be such a mess that you handle it poorly. Or maybe you just handle it poorly from the start.

These crucial conversations become extremely important when facing key life decisions. I remember reading some of Stephen Covey's work that said there are just a few defining events in a person's life that make all the difference. Each alternative at these decision points will send you in significantly different directions. Do I stay in my current job, search for a new job, or go get my MBA? Robert Frost's famous poem "The Road Not Taken" springs to mind and that is precisely the metaphor Covey uses. The road not taken prevents discovering and experiencing everything along that road.

I once had a conversation with a mortgage banker that was a crucial conversation, although I didn't understand that at the time.

It was very important to our family. By qualifying for the loan, my wife and I would have been able to buy our very first house. With too small of a loan, we would have had to compromise down to a lesser house or a location less desirable. Either of these would have changed our lifestyle, our commute, our neighborhood, and our future friends. This was one of the "roads not taken" situations and the stakes were high.

We had no formal control over the lender. We had talked with a few of them and they had different opinions about our ability to pay for the loan amount we requested. We finally applied with the one that seemed to give us the best chance of getting our loan.

The lender was driven by ratios and numbers, all designed to help them make a very rational decision. We knew the numbers said one thing, but we were willing to work hard and advance our careers to be financially able to pay off the loan. We had higher emotional stakes than the lender. Indeed, the lender's emotions were opposite of ours, not excited at all about loaning us money. They wanted to make sure they did not make a loan that would not be repaid.

After the initial loan application and a few conversations, it started looking like the lender was going to deny our loan. We became rather vocal and somewhat emotional. I was very insistent and *knew* our potential so I didn't need any banker working his formulas to say we were just the same as all the other people whose situations drove the formulas. I was adamant we could do it.

We ended up at an impasse. I didn't know about "crucial conversations" at that time of my life but I certainly felt like the situation was crucial. We decided to take a calmer approach and started to talk off the record with the lender. We explained what my wife and I were trying to achieve. The lender laid out the true risk factors from his perspective. Then we mutually started to work on how to minimize his risk while maximizing the dollar value of our loan. We couldn't close the financial gap entirely, but we did close the philosophical gap and ended up having relatives co-sign on the mortgage. They knew and believed in us, too, and the co-signing protected the lender. It was a win-win.

The lender was clearly the leader in these negotiations, but by showing yes-you yes-now leadership, we were able to find the better way for us all.

When You Have a Bad Leader

"The bad leader is hated by the people; the good leader is loved by the people; the great leader leaves them saying, 'We did it ourselves.'" [65]

—Lao-Tzu, Chinese proverb

It can be most difficult and awkward to find yourself on a team with a bad leader. But if you have come to that realization, you have already taken an important step towards improvement. Many people are too close to the situation or too weak as a follower to be able to assess the strengths and weaknesses of their formal leader.

The characterization of a person as "bad leader" is obviously a broad generalization. History is full of stories about leaders who were unsuccessful due to bad behaviors, some illegal, some immoral, and some just ineffective. Think for a moment about formal leaders you have read about in history books and newspapers. Then think about formal leaders in your own life (teachers, coaches, family members, bosses at work) who have exhibited an inability to lead in a traditional way, let alone recognizing the power of the yes-you yes-now leadership style.

There are many examples, and they all include actions and behaviors that detract from the overall goals and objectives of the team. Some examples, like the sexual misconduct episode between former U.S. President Bill Clinton and Monica Lewinsky, are events that distract a president and nation from its business as they focus instead on the bad behaviors. In some cases, a leader may have a much distorted view of what is important, which influences the basic goals of the group. Some examples of this are political dictators like Adolf Hitler or Idi Amin, whose distorted views built societies that weren't sustainable.

If you're in a situation with a bad leader in your workplace or on a team, how do you, as a follower, become aware of the misdirection of your leader? And even more important, what do you do about it?

⌖

Two brief stories illustrate possible ways to handle a bad leader situation. One is of a good leader hurting the team with bad behavior. The other is of a leader whose actions were questionable, depending on how one viewed the purpose of his role.

The first is a personal story in which my boss was failing to take clear and visible action with a peer of mine, Holly, who was not performing her job duties. The poor performance meant important work was not getting done. To compound matters, other team members started going around Holly, knowing that she would not get the job done. Damage was being inflicted on the organization and the costs were high. My boss was taking action, but not swiftly and decisively.

Seeing the expanding shock waves of damage from Holly's non-performance and then the cost of people building extra side processes to go around Holly made it clear that I had to do something. Let me tell you that my emotional bias was to dismiss Holly as soon as possible. The breadth and depth of her non-performance was so large that simply documenting it and telling her requirements for improvement would have been a straight-forward task. In fact, my boss actually did some of this, but it lacked a strong, clear action plan.

I had to come up with a way to effectively convince my boss the extent of the damage that was being done to the organization. Worse yet, I had to tell him his own reputation was being dam-aged. People were questioning his ability to take swift, decisive action. I cited some research I had read, which said high perfor-mers are less tolerant of bosses who do not also have high per-formance. They will resign and move on to another organization. Over time, an overly tolerant leader then ends up with a staff of mediocre performers – people who like a lower standard of per-formance and who like a boss who is tolerant of such perfor-mance.

To my surprise, he said he was feeling the pressure to do something and his awareness had been raised by my comments. He did eventually fire her but it took a long time and was costly to our team. A major project spun out of control with cost over-runs and unhappy customers. A few more people lost their jobs and were replaced by people with political connections, but no real interest in or ability to lead the project team. That resulted in many more staff departures and the grapevine spreading the "don't work *there*" message throughout the community.

My speaking up helped my boss better understand the situation as viewed by the larger team and, with that understanding, enabled him to take action.

The second example is about a high school basketball team. What happened on that team is either good or bad depending on your definition of the purpose and goals of a high school basketball team.

Over a period of many years, the players on this team and their fans were allowed by the coach to taunt opponents and swear at opposing coaches and even sometimes at their own coach – which he tolerated. And during games, this team's coach would act like a cheerleader to the crowd when his frenzied emotions peaked.

The coach also allowed these high school athletes to stay in their opponent's gym long after the game was over bragging about their superior play, then yelling and screaming foul language from their team bus as they drove away. The coach did nothing.

Now you might wonder if anyone associated with the team would be willing and able to see this and take action to stop it. Or you might wonder where the parents of these schoolchildren were. Surprisingly, many parents played right into the behavior, either by not paying attention, by noticing the rudeness but looking the other way, or by allowing it with a wink and a nod.

But there were a few who had intense child-parent discussions about whether or not to continue to play in such a setting. Some of them chose to play but not to participate in the name-calling and obscene language. They managed themselves. Others decided to withdraw from that environment and play other sports. In any case, they behaved as yes-you yes-now leaders by taking actions to deal with the environment the coach had allowed.

From this you can see that if you define success as winning and having rowdy behavior, then the end justifies the means. If you define success as doing the best you can do, winning, and molding young people to behave and be respectful of others, the means drives to the end. Unfortunately, the "coach-is-in-charge" structure of team sports made it difficult for good followers to change the team culture. Based on their own internal and family values, they could either behave appropriately despite the coach's example or choose to leave the team. Which are sometimes the only choices of a yes-you yes-now leader.

As with most such situations, time and truth eventually prevailed and the questionable coach was fired.

Who Makes the Decision?

"In my house, I'm the boss. My wife is just the decision maker."[66]
—Woody Allen, actor, author, movie director

Decisions to change direction are frequently made within a team working to achieve a goal. They vary in magnitude from those requiring very little information to those requiring a large body of facts; from those affecting one or two people on the team, to those affecting the direction of the entire team. Sometimes these decisions are so fundamental that they may have a bearing on the ultimate odds of the team's success or failure.

When Ed Mahler was leading the computer-based expert systems group at DuPont during the heyday of artificial intelligence in the 1990s, he would pick up a pen and ask, "What made this pen end up looking like it does and working the way it works?" People would answer with statements about the types of plastics and metals used in its construction, about the design of the ink cartridge, about the shape and form of the barrel.

While from a physical perspective these were correct answers, Mahler maintained that each and every decision – about those materials, about the target market, about the conditions in which the pen would be used, about the distribution channels – was key in making that pen what it was. And the number of decisions for a simple pen was huge.

In that situation, as well as any other team endeavor, the sheer number and magnitude of choices makes it obvious that the leader will not, and cannot, be making all the decisions. Yes-you yes-now leaders must learn their role and when it is not only appropriate, but essential, for them make the decisions which will lead to team success.

∂∞∂

The 2003 collegiate football season for the Washington State University Cougars ended on a high note, with a win over 5th ranked Texas in the Holiday Bowl. The Cougars came into the game ranked 13th in the nation and few people gave them much hope of beating the Texas Longhorns. Within the Holiday Bowl game, there were many football statistics cited for the Cougar domination of Texas. But the real strength of this team came much earlier in the season and had its roots nearly a year before.

The 2002 Cougars had done well, playing in the Rose Bowl before nearly 100,000 fans in Southern California and millions on the national television broadcast. But only a few weeks before that January 1 game, their head coach, Mike Price, announced he was leaving Washington State to become head coach at Alabama. Amid plenty of second-guessing about his reasons for leaving, he stayed with the Cougars to coach in the Rose Bowl before heading off to Tuscaloosa and his new job.

Bill Doba, a longtime Cougar assistant coach, was named the new head coach. This was a clear stability factor, but also a choice that many wondered about because the university could have done a national search.

Not long after his departure, Mike Price was entangled in allegations of off-field actions which led to his being fired as coach of the Alabama Crimson Tide before he had even held a practice with the team.

With all these distractions, Washington State opened the 2003 season picked to finish near the bottom of the Pac-10 Conference. Another disadvantage for the Cougars was a senior quarterback who had seen very little playing time.

The team surprised everyone by playing strong and tough, and by mid-season had lost only one game – an overtime loss at Notre Dame by the margin of one field goal.

With the team playing well, both the offensive and defensive units were doing their part; each supporting and compensating for the other when either unit faltered. True team spirit inspired all the players' efforts, including the quarterback, Matt Kegel.

As the season progressed, Kegel took a number of hard tackles, leaving first one shoulder, then the other, very tender and sore. It was hard for him to zip his passes like they needed to zip, and his mobility was limited by a knee injury. After one game he said, "If I get hit on that shoulder the way it is right now, it could be six months before I'm able to use that arm again because all those tendons would completely tear and my collarbone will be sticking up into my skin and it isn't going to be pretty."

Still, each week he came out to play.

Eleven games into the season, he started a game against Arizona State. In the first half, he was throwing passes without the zip, obvious to most onlookers and especially the coaches. The decision to play or not was one Kegel had to make. He did not look to the coaches, the formal leaders, to make the call.

As he came to the sideline after a play, he walked over to the backup quarterback Josh Swogger and simply said, "Your time has come, bud," and he turned the game over to his understudy.

Sharing his thought process after the game, Kegel said he started the game "… because I wanted to see if a miracle had happened during the night." When it became clear to him that none had, he knew he could and should make the decision in the best interest of the team.

"I'm not a selfish player. I'm not going to play a game I can't play, and I've been confident in Josh all season."

It was a good decision.

Coach Bill Doba said after the game, "Kegel is a great competitor and he wants whatever is best for the program. He is a very unselfish man. I'm very proud of him."

With Josh Swogger at the helm, Washington State won the game, which helped the Cougars climb into the Holiday Bowl match-up with Texas. The victory over the Longhorns gave the Cougars eighth place in the final national ranking. The key to their season-long success was the decision of a yes-you yes-now leader who was dedicated to the goals of the team.

There Go My People

Mahatma Gandhi is quoted saying, "There go my people – I must catch them for I am their leader." Visualize for a moment, the sight of a group of people walking off to go do something and leaving their leader behind, running to catch up.

In that scene, the people have a very clear idea about what they need to accomplish and how they are going to do it. They have become a strong unit and do not need to be led or even told to go take care of their business.

You may have experienced the power of yes-you yes-now leadership and felt the enormous energy from a group focused on achieving their mission. This is the highest form of teamwork and the purest form of yes-you yes-now leadership. It's important to realize that good followers are not loyal to a leader, but are loyal to the purpose. When this takes root, people are empowered to go off and get the job done.

అం∽ఆ

Over many years, De La Salle High School's football team had won a lot of games during the tenure of Coach Bob Ladoceur. Two hundred and eighty-seven wins at one point, against 14 losses and one tie. During that same time span, the team won 16 league titles. There is no doubt that they had many good players because a private school draws its student body from a large geographical area. It would be easy to say that's why they've been so good. But it would be too easy.

Coach Ladoceur developed a strong program that would have made any teacher of any subject beam. While many high schools struggle to field a varsity team due to low turnout numbers and may have only a partial schedule for a junior varsity team, De La Salle has a full schedule for the varsity, the junior varsity, *and* the freshman team.

What is so unusual about this football program? It's the team unity and focus on improving that comes from the followers, not the formal leaders.

Players are attracted to go there because the team has an intensity not found at other schools. One player said the energy he sensed during a tour in the 8th grade made him decide to go to De La Salle. That energy came from the players working out, not some coach cracking the whip.

In a 2004 Sports Illustrated feature article, the team is observed working out "in a small, poorly ventilated weight room tucked into the back of the school, [where] three dozen boys are training with a ferocious intensity. While half the group rotates among a crowded assortment of barbells and hand weights, the other half is moving through an exacting circuit of push-ups, sit-ups, and other calisthenics on a walkway between the gym and weight room. Every so often a young man supervising the workouts blows a whistle, and the boys, sweat soaking their white T-shirts and green gym shorts, hustle to the next station. Because his charges continually urge one another to keep up the tempo, the supervisor has little more to do."

How did this happen? The team, coaches and players alike, committed to a high level of success in January for a football season that had its first game in September. Players participated in optional workouts that soon became required, not by the coaches but by the players themselves. They sent the message to their teammates and to themselves – if you want to play for De La Salle, you better keep up. You better work hard to make yourself better and the team better. Players that did not want to work that hard usually went to another high school, missing out on the intense relationships and high achievement of a hard working team.

At De La Salle, the followers assumed the leadership role of driving high performance while the coaches set the framework for achieving goals. A perfect model for any organization.

Conclusion

Leading Yourself, Your Team, and Your Leader

"On every team there is a core group who sets the tone for everyone else. If the tone is positive, you have half the battle won. If it is negative, you are beaten before you even walk out on the field."[68]

Chuck Noll, former coach of the Pittsburgh Steelers,
winners of four Super Bowls

The ideas in this book are tools to be used in the spirit of achieving team goals. They give you power from where you are now. You don't need to be promoted. You don't need to go back to school. You don't need to wait for anything. You can practice yes-you yes-now leadership today. Yes you! Yes now! No excuses.

In its simplest form, a follower shares in the purpose or goal of others. How and when the shared purpose is established will vary but it is clear that nothing gets done without followers doing most of the work. Construction supervisors don't wield a hammer, their teammates on the job site do. Basketball coaches don't shoot the ball, their players on the court do. When everyone contributes, amazing things happen.

Yes-you yes-now leadership is not something laid out in a recipe. There aren't ten steps to becoming a yes-you yes-now leader because the role of the follower and leader is a constantly changing human dynamic. That is why so many of the topics in this book are about human dynamics from the perspective of the follower, who can simply choose to be a yes-you yes-now leader.

What can be more fundamental in human dynamics than seeking to understand yourself through self-awareness, coupled with seeking to understand others by asking questions?

If this were all done in a world with well-intentioned people, it would be so easy. But there are the bad leaders who assert themselves and an effective follower must counter them. Doing so can be very difficult, if not done with a focus on team goals. This is why it so important to have loyalty to the goals and not to the leader. Leaders will come and go but the goals will not. It is still the work of the team to win the games, to surpass sales goals, or to finish projects regardless of how many formal leaders come and go.

When a team learns to function as a single unit, intent on achieving goals, they begin to make real progress. *Hoosiers*, the movie dramatization of the small high school that won the Indiana State Basketball Championship in 1954, showed a team playing together with fewer athletes than many teams. The smaller single unit was more powerful than a larger fragmented team as the basketball season moved along.

When a team performs under adverse conditions, no matter what the cause, stress can take its toll. In these situations it is important for a yes-you yes-now leader to step up and contribute to holding the team together. Within each individual and within the group of individuals, stress will reveal true capabilities. It is easy to look good and feel good when everything is going well. When they're not, each person is tested to see if they will crumble or rise to the challenge.

Personal growth comes when a person chooses to put the greater good before one's own good, driven by a sense of duty to the group goals. As David Rockefeller learned, that sense of duty provides the stage on which a person can develop skills and abilities that would have otherwise remained dormant.

Sometimes the group goals seem impossible. How could humans go to the moon by the end of the 1960s when they first went into space in the late 1950s? U.S. President John F. Kennedy's speech in 1961 that launched the American moon program seemed farfetched until, step-by-step, thousands of people adopted the moon landing goal as their own.

Followership has been important as long as people have joined together to accomplish tasks that are so large and complex that no one person could possibly do them alone. These are tasks that, in the modern world, truly make a difference between the status quo and breakthrough achievements, whether it is going to the moon or eradicating a disease.

These are noble ambitions beyond themselves because in addition to achieving a goal, they form the basis of social cooperation that is also noble, leveraging each member of the team as their skills are needed. Everyone can contribute and everyone can succeed when they practice yes-you yes-now leadership.

Appendix: The Voices of Children

Daniel Goleman, the author of the landmark book *Emotional Intelligence* once said, "If your emotional abilities aren't in hand, if you don't have self-awareness, if you are not able to manage your distressing emotions, if you can't have empathy and have effective relationships, then no matter how smart you are, you are not going to get very far."[69]

Part of being a yes-you yes-now leader is self-awareness. As we move into adulthood, we may lose our ability to assess ourselves. Young people are better able to take a fresh look to see how they contribute to interactions with their friends, schoolmates, and teammates. They may try to blame someone else at first but when asked to think about their contributions to conflict, they are often more forthright than adults. This section looks at yes-you yes-now leadership from the perspective of young people, both grade school and high school ages, with the intent of showing how simple it all is – if you can be clear with yourself.

Most of us have great difficulty judging and assessing ourselves accurately because if we do, we may see something we don't like. And seeing something we don't like means we have to change, and change is hard and painful. But not for children.

Grade School Children

Children around the age of ten give excellent commentary on things in their world and sometimes in yours, too. By this age their brains have developed enough to make clear observations about the world. Yet they are not so inhibited by social pressures to sugar-coat what they tell you. They give you their usually well-formed thoughts with directness and without malice. It is just what they see.

A number of grade school children from first through sixth grades were asked to name a word or a phrase describing something about a person with whom they would like to work. This is what they came up with.

Listening	Communicating	Responsible
Dependable	Truthful	Has authority
Trustworthy	Be kind	Accept requests
Be organized	Be dedicated	Be patient
Cooperation	Be friendly	Nice
Don't quit	Ideas	Role model
Smart	Respected	Always on task
Diplomatic	Understanding	Asserting
Quick thinking		

Quite a list! If all the team members on our teams at work exhibited these characteristics, can you imagine how much easier it would be to work together? In fact, it's impossible to have all these characteristics in one team because some of them may oppose each other. Being truthful and nice is a hard combination for many people when there is bad news to deliver. And other characteristics such as too much friendliness at the expense of staying on task, would lead to no achievement if taken to the extreme.

These children were sufficiently self-aware to realize their own limitations when they scored themselves on each characteristic and provided a sentence or two explaining their score. Every one of these is insightful to adults, as well as children. The scoring scale was 1 to 5, with 5 the best and the comments are presented unedited, as written by the students. It is worth taking the time to read a few and reflect on them.

Listening

"4¾   I am good at listening to friend's problems then making them feel better."

"4½   Sometimes I am not good at listening because I am talking."

"4   I am a very good listener because I almost always listen to my friends problems but occasionally I'll walk out when my parents talk."

"2   I'm not very good at listening to others. I may have an idea but I need work on listening more than just thinking my idea is the best."

Communicating

"4¾ I don't know why I think that but Madison thinks so too." From Alyssa (see Madison's comment below).

"4½   When I talk I get my point through 95% of the time but rarely I get lost and start going off on something else."   We should be so lucky for this to happen only rarely.

"4   Very few times will I ever be misunderstood."
That's a stretch goal.
"3½ Do I communicate well? I'm not sure but Alyssa
thinks I do." From Madison.

Responsible
"4   I haven't forgotten my homework this year but
sometimes I misplace things."
"3   I can take a bit of responsibility but sometimes its
so much for me I don't do it."
"2¾ Many times when I have something to do that will
affect everyone, I leave it to the last minute."

Dependable
"5   At school I help teachers out every week and I've
showed up everytime unless I <u>HAVE</u> to stay in and do
work or I'm sick."

Truthful
"5   I am so truthful! I sometimes do quite fib but I
think I get a 5 because I have a streak of a month without
lying."
"5   I have told only one lie in my life and it was about a
tree that I thought was bleeding."
"3   I almost always tell the truth but every once in a
while I'll sneak some Halloween candy."
"3   I always help my friends when they're hurt & I let
them chose what to play."

Has Authority
"4   I have a lot of respect at my school but when I ask
them to stop some smart alicky kids keep it up."

Trustworthy

"4¾ I really never tell anybodys secret unless if it was something sierius like if they had a really bad cut or something like that."

Be kind

"4¾ I am friendly so I must be pretty kind."

"4 I always help my friends when they're hurt and I let them choose what to play."

"2 I usaly have a really hard time cooperating and get into a fight that is usaly unnecessary. I very rarely get along because I am picky and stubborn."

Accept requests

"3 I gave myself a 3 because I am stubborn. I like to go with my own ideas."

Be organized

"3 Because I usually avoid cleaning and organising. Only if I am playing maid will I clean-organise."

Be dedicated

"3½ Sometimes in groups when I am the leader I will not do what I have dedicated myself to."

"2½ I tend to give up on things, like needlepoint easily but in school I almost never give up."

"2 I have started many things but quit later. I have started wonderful books, karate, and other things."

Be patient

"3½ I get impatient for things like road trips and I am grumpy for a while."

"3 I vary if I am patient. It usaly depends on what I'm waiting for. Usaly, I want things to get over with."

Cooperation
"3 I am sort of good at cooperation and sometimes not."

Be friendly
"5 I try to make friends with everyone I meet or know. I have all sorts of friends."
"4½ Am I friendly? I hope so. It's hard to rate yourself on that."
"4 I do yell at people but a lot of the time I do talk nice, try to solve their problems, and share."

Nice
"3 Sometimes I am nice about things or else I am in a totally different mood."

Don't quit
"5 I only quit if told or the problem is impossible."

Ideas
"5 I am always good at coming up with ideas. Sometimes I think up too many and get in trouble."

Role model
"3 Sometimes I am either not acting correctly or I don't do things right."

Smart

"4 Usually I am smart but sometimes my action leads to an accident or big trouble."

Respected

"4 People respect me because I have the ability to listen and come up with good ideas."

"3½ When I am playing a game I don't like I stay in the game for my friends if they like it."

Always on task

"2½ I almost always stop working to look around."

Diplomatic

"5 I always get the deal and I know what to say and when to say it. Also I never say something bad to someone higher in authority."

Understanding

"3½ Many times in a group I can understand their problems. Also at times I get annoyed and harsh."

Asserting

"2½ Many times people will easily use power over me."

Quick thinking

"4 In a group I can think of a solution fast enough but sometimes the group will be stalled."

These grade school children speak plainly and honestly about their fellow followers, their interactions, and group dynamics. We can learn a lot about our own teams, which get bogged down in more complex social dynamics – or at least we pretend they do!

ॐ

High School Students

Let's now see how an older group of students view their group dynamics. See if you notice a change in perspective. Is it more accurate? Do these more mature views help or hurt their team? Or do you think they have a lot to learn about the real world?

As students near high school graduation, they are young adults in many ways, prepared to make decisions with independence. They have spent many years in group situations, from the classroom to debate, music, theater, or sports teams.

While they have learned the social protocol missing in ten-year-olds, they still retain a clear and penetrating view of how followers behave, either to achieve or to block achievement of a goal.

For this group of people, I asked questions in four areas.

1. On a group project at school did a leader take charge? Did everyone follow? How did it work out (or not)? Did anyone slack? Why or why not? What do you think would have made it work perfectly?

2. Think of a group or team. What makes a good follower?
3. Why are the skills you listed important? What do they add to team success?
4. Do you spend more time in a follower or a leader role? How much of each?

Their answers are sometimes predictable but often surprising and thought provoking. The comments are presented unedited, as written by the students. Here is what they had to say.

On a group project at school did a leader take charge? Did everyone follow? How did it work out (or not)? Did anyone slack? Why or why not? What do you think would have made it work perfectly?

"A leader always stepped forward and took charge and usually everyone followed because we wanted a good grade. When people slacked off, they felt someone else would do their work for them, so the project would have worked better if their was an individual grade that went along with the group grade."

"Yes, someone took charge. Most everyone followed but there are always those one or two people that don't put their share of effort in. Ideas were brainstormed and certain people wouldn't participate with feedback or input. I think there were slackers because their view on school might be different than ones willing to work for a good grade. It might all work better if teams are chosen by the people on the teams."

"Usually a leader took charge to organize and make sure everything got done. Everyone followed because they agreed on what needed to be done, though there were some problems when deciding how to do it. People slacked because they didn't take personal responsibility and thought someone else would take care of the work. It would have worked perfectly if everyone carried their load."

"A leader always took charge but not everyone followed. But the leader still tried to get everyone involved and didn't let one or two people hold the team back. There were slackers because it is especially hard to have one of your peers be your leader but that is your decision to look at it that way. It would have all worked better if everyone just got stuff done and didn't care who got credit."

"Someone took charge because it helps when someone in a group does, as long as they are willing to incorporate other people's ideas as well. Most people followed and the leader would say if anyone is opposed to an idea, they could say why and we would try to make a compromise. Some people in the group slacked because they thought it was 'cool' not to do anything. It would have been perfect if everyone contributed because we'd have more thing to choose from, making it easier on everyone. Also no one would feel left out or like they didn't help with it."

Think of a group or team. What makes a good follower?

"An important ability for a follower is to not always needing to be in the spotlight."

"Listening skills and patience are two very important traits of a follower. Also being able to go with the flow [pick your battles, not everything needs your imprint] and making something not so great seem a bit better."

"Give all of your effort, sincerely working your hardest – even when no one is watching – to do what needs to be done. Help your teammates."

"Be patient, have good listening skills, be good at whatever they are in charge of, have commitment to their team, work as hard as everyone. Honest is good too."

"Character, maturity, willingness to do the small things, determination to succeed, and intellect."

Why are the skills you listed important? What do they add to team success?

"All the follower skills are important because there can be only one leader at a time. This leaves more than half of the team with a follower role. In order to make a strong team, everyone needs to be able to adapt to different roles."

"Follower skills are important because not everyone can be the leader, that would only lead to drama. Followers add completeness to the team and make more of a happy environment. Everyone has a job on a team, and if everyone goes through with their job then only good things can happen."

"Good followers on a team makes sure no one will leave anything undone or not done well."

"A group needs follower skills in order to succeed and if the leader cannot even demonstrate some of those skills, it will be hard for the rest of the team to be successful. Someone needs to set good examples."

"You have to be a bigger person to show those skills and it is not easy, but you do it and people have a reason to look up to you."

Do you spend more time in a follower or a leader role? How much of each?

"I spend about half and half. I don't follow someone or something if I don't agree. However, I will follow if there is a good idea, concept, or opinion."

"I would say about 50% leader, 50% follower. I like to go with the team flow yet I'm not afraid to step up and voice my opinion."

"70% leader, 30% follower"

"I try to remain in the middle but am so involved it is hard to tell. I really like to listen to other people's ideas and build off of them."

"Leader about two thirds of the time, follower about a third."

There are themes running through the comments of these young adults. They are very much aware of personal aspects of following and leading, with comments on core expertise, personal responsibility, perseverance through good and bad times, and that it is good to find out why people are on your team – what's in it for them – and if that is aligned with the team.

The students commented on the importance of both the team and the process to resolve conflict. They don't care who gets credit, as long as the goal is reached but they want the freedom to choose what works for the team. And to keep the team going, they want role clarity and consequences for not performing.

Among the follower and leader roles, the personal and the team dynamics, they want synergy by having input to group processes and having their voices heard. They see the value of aligning individuals with the team, culminating in the power of a common goal.

It's interesting to note that most people think they are in a leadership role more often than not. Though the roles of leader and follower may constantly be shifting, most people are indeed practicing yes-you yes-now leadership. Perhaps this is a phenomena similar to "I'm a good driver; it's everyone else on the road you better watch out for."

In the big picture, it takes everyone on the road and everyone on the team to cooperate for the greater good. If traffic laws and controls are well-designed and drivers comply, everyone gets to their destination on time. Both groups of students seem to understand that good followers have self-awareness of their contributions to this greater good and do not blame the others, always looking to smooth the flow.

About the author

Steven C. Tarr learned the power of yes-you yes-now leadership in both his executive roles and front-line jobs. He progressed to become a top executive in high technology companies and leading-edge health care institutions, first seeing the value of effective following early in his working life by cleaning offices, delivering newspapers, stocking grocery shelves, programming computers, and eventually leading large teams of people. In each case, he has been both a leader and a follower, learning to work with others to achieve team goals. He earned his undergraduate and master's degrees from Washington State University and his doctorate from Portland State University. He enjoys volunteer coaching high school basketball and seeing the growth of people, young and old, as they persevere to achieve more than they thought possible.

Notes

[1] Leadership Quotes, University of Arizona Cooperative Extension, http://*cals*.arizona.edu/extension/leadership/quotes.html, 3 April 2002.

[2] Charles Mackay, *A Thousand and One Gems of English Prose*, (London: George Routledge and Sons, 1872) 521.

[3] Brent Kelley, at golf.about.com/od/golfersmen/p/tom_watson.htm.

[4] Mark Stefik, "Fast Talk: Mother (and Fathers) of Invention," *Fast Company* February 2004: 45.

[5] John Wooden, *Practical Modern Basketball*, (New York: Macmillan, 1988), 13.

[6] George W. Bush, "President Honors 2003 Presidential Medal of Freedom Recipients," The White House, Washington, D.C., July 23, 2003.

[7] John Wooden, *Practical Modern Basketball*, (New York: Macmillan, 1988), 13.

[8] John Wooden, *Wooden: A Lifetime of Observations and Reflections On and Off the Court*, (Chicago: Contemporary Books, 1997) 44.

[9] Colin Powell, *My American Journey*, (New York: Random House, 1995) 318.

[10] See sports illustrated.

[11] Donna Karan at www.brainyquote.com/quotes/quotes/d/donnakaran186048.html.

[12] Richard Battin, "Some Funny Things Happened on the Way to the Moon," American Institute of Aeronautics and Astronautics 27th Aerospace Sciences Meeting, Reno, Nevada, 9 January 1989.

[13] Colin Powell, *My American Journey*, (New York: Random House, 1995) 167.

[14] The City of Santa Clarita Celebrates the Six Pillars of Character, http://www.santa-clarita.com/cityhall/council/julyaugust.htm, date unknown.

[15] Bertrand Russell at www.brainyquote.com/quotes/authors/b/bertrand_russell.html.

[16] Tryon Edwards, *A Dictionary of Thoughts,* (Detroit: F.B. Dickerson, 1908), 525

[17] J. Donald Walters at thinkexist.com/quotation/self-acceptance_comes_from_meeting_life-s/326442.html.

[18] Michael Kinsley, "Blogged Down," *The Washington Post*, 19 December 2004, B7.

[19] Josh Billings at en.proverbia.net/citastema.asp?tematica=1076.

[20] Bill Madden, "Zimmer Insists His Days In Pinstripes Are Really Over," *New York Daily News*, 26 October 2003.

[21] Alice Munro at thinkexist.com/quotes/alice_munro.

[22] unknown origin.

[23] Mischel, W., Shoda, Y., & Rodriguez, M. L. "Delay of gratification in children," *Science, 26 May 1989*, 933-938.

[24] Roy Rivenburg, "Our 'instant-gratification' culture often makes it tough to resist temptation," *The Seattle Times* 20 April 2004.

[25] Roy E. Disney at ThinkExist.com.

[26] Barry Schwartz, "The Tyranny of Choice," *Scientific American* April 2004.

[27] Rick Wakeman at www.brainyquote.com/quotes/authors/r/rick_wakeman.html.

[28] Kobe Bryant at www.brainyquote.com/quotes/quotes/k/kobebryant167164.html.

[29] Ronald Blum, "Yanks vs. Red Sox: Same old ending," *USA Today* 16 October 2003.

[30] Arthur Wellesley at www.historyhome.co.uk/c-eight/france/welly.htm.

[31] Carly Fiorina, "Commencement Address – North Carolina A&T University," May 7, 2005, Greensboro, North Carolina.

[32] William Shatner as Edwin Poole, *Boston Legal*, ABC Television, 2006.

[33] Billie Jean King at www.brainyquote.com/quotes/authors/b/billie_jean_king.html.

[34] Allen Klein, "Humor and September 11th," at www.allenklein.com/articles/humor9-11part1.htm.

[35] Ryan Underwood, "60 Seconds on Doing the Impossible," *Fast Company* March 2005: 32.

[36] Carly Fiorina, interviewed by Louise Kehoe, *Commonwealthclub*, 21 July 2003.

[37] George Bernhard Shaw at ThinkExist.com.

[38] John Sutherland, "Joy, Precision from Eroica, Prague Orchestra," *The Seattle Times* 23 October 2003.

[39] www.dallaschambermusic.org/the-eroica-trio, 2003.

[40] Gwendolyn Freed, "Music Hath Charms, All Showing," *The Wall Street Journal* 18 August 1998: www.wsj.com.

[41] John Wooden, *Wooden: A Lifetime of Observations and Reflections On and Off the Court*, (Chicago: Contemporary Books, 1997) 78.

[42] JK Rowling, *Harry Potter and the Chamber of Secrets*, (New York: Scholastic, 2000).

[43] Alexander Graham Bell at www.brainyquote.com/quotes/quotes/a/alexanderg390037.html.

[44] Colin Powell, *My American Journey*, (New York: Random House, 1995) 59.

[45] Mission Statement of De La Salle High School, Concord, California, USA. www.dlsh.org.

[46] Pearl S. Buck at thinkexist.com/quotes/pearl_s._buck/.

[47] J.G. Holland at www.brainyquote.com/quotes/authors/j/j_g_holland.html.

[48] Thomas Szasz at www.quotationspage.com/quotes/Thomas_Szasz/.

[49] Kareem Abdul-Jabbar at www.teambuildinginc.com/popups/team_quips.htm.

[50] Peter Drucker at www.quotesandsayings.com/gmistakes1.htm.

[51] Patrick Goldstein, "When film executives show moral responsibility," *The Seattle Times* 29 November 2003.

[52] Gene Hackman as Norman Dale, *Hoosiers*, DeHaven Productions/MGM/Orion Pictures, 1986.

[53] Bob Finnigan, "Mariners bust loose," *The Seattle Times* 13 April 2006.

[54] Colin Powell, *My American Journey*, (New York: Random House, 1995) 56.

[55] Colin Powell, *My American Journey*, (New York: Random House, 1995) 320.

[56] Elliot Jacques at www.cybernation.com/victory/quotations/authors/quotes_jaques_elliot.html.

[57] John Wooden, "Ten Burning Questions for John Wooden," espn.go.com/page2/s/questions/wooden.html, 2001.

[58] David Rockefeller, *Memoirs*, (New York: Random House, 2003), 106.

[59] David Rockefeller, *Memoirs*, (New York: Random House, 2003), 106-107.

[60] Gene Kranz, *Failure Is Not an Option* (New York: Berkeley, 2000) 106.

[61] Oscar Hammerstein, "Getting to Know You," *The King and I*, 1956.

[62] Gene Kranz, *Failure Is Not an Option* (New York: Berkeley, 2000) 105.

[63] Colin Powell, *My American Journey*, (New York: Random House, 1995) 144.

[64] Kerry Patterson, Joseph Grenny, Ron McMillan, Al Switzler, *Crucial Conversations*, (New York: McGraw-Hill), 2002.

[65] Many versions exist. This is paraphrased from http://thinkexist.com/quotes/lao_tzu/2.html

[66] Woody Allen at /thinkexist.com/quotes/woody_allen.

[67] Colin Powell, *My American Journey*, (New York: Random House, 1995) 194.

[68] Chuck Knoll at http://www.powerbasketball.com/060721.html

[69] Daniel Goleman at www.brainyquote.com/quotes/authors/d/daniel_goleman.html.

CPSIA information can be obtained at www.ICGtesting.com
Printed in the USA
BVOW05s1621240615

405981BV00001B/41/P